Pathfinder®Guides

Cheshire

Walks

*Originally compiled by
Brian Conduit
Revised by Neil Coates*

Text: Brian Conduit
                        Revised text Neil Coates
Photography: Brian Conduit and Neil Coates
Editorial: Ark Creative (UK) Ltd
Design: Ark Creative (UK) Ltd

ISBN: 978-1-85458-567-7

While every care has been taken to ensure the accuracy of the route directions, the publishers cannot accept responsibility for errors or omissions, or for changes in details given. The countryside is not static: hedges and fences can be removed, field boundaries can alter, footpaths can be rerouted and changes in ownership can result in the closure or diversion of some concessionary paths. Also, paths that are easy and pleasant for walking in fine conditions may become slippery, muddy and difficult in wet weather, while stepping stones across rivers and streams may become impassable.

If you find an inaccuracy in either the text or maps, please write to Crimson Publishing at the address below.

First published 2003 by Jarrold Publishing
Revised and reprinted 2007, 2009, 2011.

This edition first published in Great Britain 2011 by Crimson Publishing, a division of:
Crimson Business Ltd,
Westminster House, Kew Road, Richmond, Surrey, TW9 2ND
www.totalwalking.co.uk

Printed in Singapore. 5/11

A catalogue record for this book is available from the British library.

Front cover: Teggs Nose
Previous page: Quarry Bank Mill

Contents

Approximate walk times

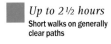 *Up to 2½ hours*
Short walks on generally
clear paths

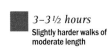 *3–3½ hours*
Slightly harder walks of
moderate length

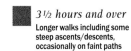 *3½ hours and over*
Longer walks including some
steep ascents/descents,
occasionally on faint paths

*The walk times are provided as a guide only and are calculated using an average walking
speed of 2½mph (4km/h), adding one minute for each 10m (33ft) of ascent, and then
rounding the result to the nearest half hour.*

Walks are considered to be dog friendly unless specified.

SCALE 1:357 000 or 1 INCH to about 5¾ MILES *1CM to 3.5KM*

KILOMETRES

MILES

KEYMAP HEIGHTS SHOWN IN METRES

At-a-glance

Walk	Page	Start	Nat. Grid Reference	Distance	Time	Height Gain
Above Helsby and Frodsham	68	Helsby	SJ 490749	7 miles (11.3km)	3 ½ hrs	870ft (265m)
Astbury Mere and village	28	Astbury Mere Country Park	SJ 846627	5½ miles (8.8km)	2½ hrs	215ft (65m)
Audlem and the Shropshire Union Canal	32	Audlem	SJ 659436	5¾ miles (9.2km)	2½ hrs	130ft (40m)
Beeston Castle and the Shropshire Union Canal	58	Beeston Castle	SJ 540590	6½ miles (10.5km)	3 hrs	425ft (130m)
Bollington and Nab Head	14	Bollington	SJ 930780	3¾ miles (6km)	2 hrs	670ft (205m)
Boothsdale	26	Gresty's Waste car park	SJ 540686	5¼ miles (8.4km)	2½ hrs	690ft (210m)
Bulkeley Hill and Raw Head	34	Bulkeley	SJ 523544	5¾ miles (9.3km)	3 hrs	935ft (285m)
Caldy Hill, Thurstaston and the Wirral Way	62	Thurstaston Visitor Centre	SJ 239834	7¼ miles (11.6km)	3½ hrs	445ft (135m)
Chester and the River Dee	22	Chester	SJ 405662	5¼ miles (8.4km)	2½ hrs	165ft (50m)
Dane Valley	20	Brereton Heath Country Park	SJ 795653	5 miles (8km)	2½ hrs	330ft (100m)
Delamere Forest	30	Linmere Visitor Centre	SJ 548704	5¾ miles (9.1km)	2½ hrs	410ft (110m)
Disley and Lyme Park	40	Disley	SJ 972845	6 miles (9.6km)	3 hrs	935ft (285m)
Dunham Park and the Bridgewater Canal	43	Oldfield Brow	SJ 751888	6½ miles (10.5km)	3 hrs	n/a
The Etherow and Goyt Valleys	88	Etherow Country Park, Compstall	SJ 965908	10½ miles (16.8km)	5½ hrs	1,280ft (390m)
Farndon and Churton	49	Farndon	SJ 412543	6¼ miles (10km)	3 hrs	115ft (35m)
Gawsworth Hall and North Rode	52	Gawsworth	SJ 886694	6½ miles (10.5km)	3 hrs	295ft (90m)
Little Budworth Country Park	16	Little Budworth Country Park	SJ 590654	4 miles (6.4km)	2 hrs	n/a
Malpas	80	Malpas	SJ 487472	8½ miles (13.6km)	4 hrs	395ft (120m)
Mow Cop and Little Moreton Hall	71	Mow Cop	SJ 856573	7½ miles (12km)	3½ hrs	820ft (250m)
Sandbach	37	Sandbach	SJ 758608	6 miles (9.7km)	3 hrs	165ft (50m)
Shutlingsloe	77	Trentabank car park	SJ 961711	6½ miles (10.5km)	3½ hrs	1,280ft (390m)
Styal and the Bollin Valley	18	Styal	SJ 835835	5 miles (8km)	2½ hrs	250ft (75m)
Tegg's Nose and Macclesfield Forest	84	Tegg's Nose Country Park	SJ 950732	8½ miles (13.7km)	4½ hrs	1,855ft (565m)
Timbersbrook and The Cloud	74	Timbersbrook	SJ 894627	6½ miles (10.4km)	3½ hrs	950ft (290m)
Trent and Mersey Canal and Great Budworth	55	Marbury Country Park	SJ 652763	7 miles (11.3km)	3 hrs	260ft (80m)
Wirral Way, Parkgate and the Dee Estuary	65	Willaston	SJ 330773	8¼ miles (13.2km)	3½ hrs	245ft (75m)
Wirswall Hill and Big Mere	12	Marbury	SJ 561457	3½ miles (5.6km)	2 hrs	250ft (75m)
Wybunbury	46	Wybunbury	SJ 699498	6¼ miles (10km)	3 hrs	310ft (95m)

Comments

There are fine views across the Mersey Estuary but also some steep ascents and descents across the wooded cliffs that mark the northern end of the sandstone ridge.

The walk starts by a mere and includes a stretch of canal, field paths and an attractive village with an imposing church.

This flat walk, mostly across fields and along a canal towpath, provides open and extensive views.

The wooded sandstone ridge, crowned by both medieval Beeston Castle and the adjacent 19th-century Peckforton Castle, is the dominant landscape feature of this walk.

The short and relatively easy climb to the summit of Nab Head rewards you with grand and extensive views. A shorter option omits the climb to Nab Head.

There are attractive wooded stretches on the edge of Delamere Forest and fine views across Cheshire to the hills of North Wales.

This fine scenic walk, quite steep in places, takes you through beautiful woodland to the highest point on the sandstone ridge.

There is superb woodland and heathland and a modest climb rewards you with fine views over both the Dee and Mersey estuaries.

Attractive riverside meadows beside the Dee, coupled with Chester's numerous historic sites, makes for an absorbing walk.

An easy exploration of the peaceful Dane Valley, visiting the secluded village of Swettenham, set amid traditional meadows and host to an inspiring arboretum.

A fascinating exploration of Delamere's lakes and forest, with a superb viewpoint as a finale.

The contrasting views take in both Greater Manchester and the moorlands of the Peak District and there is a memorable stretch through Lyme Park, passing in front of the hall.

The walk makes use of both a disused railway track and a canal towpath and the highlight is a walk through Dunham Park, with fine views of the great house.

A challenging walk which discovers the woodland, ridges and moors fringing the Mersey's headwaters at the edge of the Peak District.

The opening stretch is mainly across fields between Farndon and Churton; the return leg is beside the River Dee.

Half-timbered Gawsworth Hall makes a picturesque focal point for this walk through a typical Cheshire landscape.

There are attractive wooded stretches and, towards the end, a fine view across Budworth Pool of Little Budworth Church.

The views extend over the Cheshire plain and across to the hills of North Wales on this undulating walk to the south and east of Malpas.

From the heights of Mow Cop, you descend to the Macclesfield Canal and on across fields to Little Moreton Hall. A shorter version of the walk omits the visit to Little Moreton Hall.

The first part of the walk is mainly through a secluded valley; much of the return leg is beside a canal.

A mixture of woodland and open moorland, with outstanding views, are the main ingredients of this superb Peak District walk that takes you to the distinctive summit of Shutlingsloe.

A fascinating glimpse of a 'model' Georgian industrial community is the culmination of this undulating route through the sylvan treasure of the River Bollin's gorge.

This route in the Peak District encompasses both the conifers of Macclesfield Forest and some rough moorland walking. The views are superb. Shorter version of walk 7½ miles (12km).

After walking across fields and beside a canal, the climb to the summit of The Cloud is a relatively easy one and the views are superb. Two shorter options available (4¼ and 2½ miles).

A country park, picturesque village, canal and unique – and recently restored – boatlift create a walk of great interest and variety.

Easy walking along a disused railway track is followed by an invigorating stretch beside the Dee estuary. There are fine views looking across to North Wales.

On the final stretch, there are particularly memorable views looking across Big Mere to Marbury Church.

This lengthy but undemanding walk explores the pleasant and gently undulating countryside around the hilltop village of Wybunbury.

Introduction to Cheshire

The conventional image of the typical Cheshire landscape is of rich parklands, lazily meandering rivers, tree-fringed meres, attractive black-and-white villages with sandstone churches, and flat, lush pastures occupied by contented-looking cattle. And indeed this is a largely accurate picture of much of the county. This is the landscape that has made Cheshire a major dairy farming area, noted especially for its mild, crumbly cheese. But there are other sides to Cheshire and the county is far more varied than many people realise – it is undulating rather than flat, and there are hills, even rugged ones at that. Cheshire is a frontier county, not only in the obvious sense of being on the Welsh border, but also as a frontier between south and north. Its rich pasturelands are similar to those of its neighbours to the south – Shropshire and Staffordshire – but its gritstone moors and northern industrial and commuter belt are more reminiscent of the textile country of Lancashire and Yorkshire.

Hill country

Outside the area it is perhaps not widely known that a slice of eastern Cheshire lies within the Peak District National Park. Here is a landscape of deep valleys, gritstone moors, isolated farms and stone hamlets that could not be farther removed from the typical picture of the county just described. This is Pennine Cheshire, virtually identical in appearance and spirit to the moorlands farther north in Yorkshire and Lancashire. Macclesfield is the chief centre of this part of the county and could hardly be more of a Pennine town with its skyline of silk mills and terrace houses.

Farther west – and visible from the gritstone moors of the Peak District

Primrose Lane (Walk 28)

– is another range of hills; the sandstone ridge which runs north to south across the central part of the county. These are lower and less rugged than the gritstone moors of the Peak District and largely covered with woodland but the ridge provides some surprisingly steep slopes and a number of fine viewpoints. In the south, this sandstone ridge drops gently to the Shropshire border but where it ends in the north, at the cliffs above Helsby and Frodsham, it falls away abruptly to the flat and heavily industrialised country of the Mersey Estuary.

Commuter country

Another side to Cheshire is the commuter belt area, 'stockbroker country', in the north, serving Manchester, Liverpool and the adjacent towns. To the south of Stockport and Manchester are a collection of towns and villages that are among the most affluent in the country outside the Home Counties, but still with much attractive countryside between them. Farther west, between the Dee and the Mersey, is the Wirral peninsula, just across the river from Liverpool. Despite suburban expansion and industrialisaton on its eastern Mersey side, the Wirral still retains a sense of remoteness and isolation in places and has some good walking country. Particularly impressive are the views from its western side, looking across the marshlands of the Dee to the hills of North Wales.

County boundaries

The River Mersey was always the traditional and clearly defined border between Cheshire and Lancashire but this changed in the local government reorganisation of 1974. Cheshire both gained and lost. It gained land around Warrington and Widnes, to the north of the Mersey, but lost lands in the Wirral and to the south of Manchester to the new metropolitan counties of Merseyside and Greater Manchester respectively.

For the purposes of this walking guide, the old borders of the former County Palatine have been used; thus routes partially in the current Merseyside and Greater Manchester metropolitan counties are included.

Castles, forests and country houses

Cheshire is part of the Welsh border country and in the Middle Ages the earls of Chester were given almost royal powers in exchange for protecting this vulnerable area from Welsh raids. Castles such as Beeston, Chester and the vanished one at Malpas are reminders that for many centuries this was a warlike and unsettled area.

During the Middle Ages, a substantial part of northern Cheshire was covered by the great royal forests of Mara and Mondrum and largely given over to hunting. Subsequent fellings in the 17th and 18th centuries destroyed much of these forests but a fragment survives at Delamere – excellent walking country – and there are good wooded stretches in other

Little Moreton Hall (Walk 23)

parts of the county.

The ending of the wars with the Welsh brought more peaceful and settled conditions and the subsequent agricultural prosperity was largely responsible for the handsome old towns, attractive villages and country houses for which the county is renowned. Of the latter, Little Moreton Hall is the most famous. Almost everyone has seen pictures of it on calendars and birthday cards as its picturesque appearance has made it one of the most photographed buildings in the country. It typifies Cheshire and has virtually become a symbol of the county. Other black-and-white houses are at Gawsworth and Bramhall and thousands of visitors flock to the great houses and parklands of Lyme, Adlington, Tatton and Dunham Massey, many now in the ownership of the National Trust.

Chester

The principal tourist attraction in Cheshire is the county town, the great historic city of Chester, one of England's oldest, most attractive and most distinctive cities. Originally the Roman fort of Deva, it has been a major port, fortress, base for English incursions into Wales, administrative centre and cathedral city. Its circuit of walls is virtually intact – and make a superb urban walk – and within them are the city's main historic and architectural attractions. Unique to Chester are the Rows, two-storeyed covered walkways, with shops at both street and upper level. Why these are found nowhere else has never been satisfactorily explained but it is known that they correspond with the limits of the Roman fort.

Canals and railway tracks

Although primarily an agricultural county, the Industrial Revolution did not entirely pass Cheshire by. Proximity to Manchester ensured that north-east Cheshire became part of the textile belt and the county shared with Lancashire the later chemical industries of Merseyside. Birkenhead, chief town of the Wirral, rivalled its near neighbour, Liverpool, as a port and important centre for shipbuilding. A legacy of this which is particularly relevant to walkers is the extensive canal network. There are four main canals – Macclesfield, Trent and Mersey, Bridgewater and Shropshire Union – and they were constructed both to serve Cheshire's own industries and agriculture and to provide a link between the industrial Midlands and the Mersey. Their towpaths now make excellent walking routes, tranquil and scenic.

Another legacy of the Industrial Revolution is a number of disused railway tracks and some of these are featured in the selection of walks. The medium-distance Wirral Way is based entirely around a railway line which ran along the western side of the Wirral.

Walking in the area

Cheshire has a large number of clearly waymarked recreational routes. The principal ones are the Wirral Way and the Sandstone and Gritstone Trails. The latter two run, for the most part, in a roughly north–south direction along the ridges of the sandstone hills of central Cheshire and the gritstone hills and moors of the Peak District respectively. Stretches of the South Cheshire Way, Bollin Valley Way, Dane Valley Way and Delamere Way are also featured in the routes in this book.

So if walkers come to Cheshire expecting a wholly flat county, they are in for something of a surprise. There are plenty of easy, gently undulating and undemanding walks that take you across a typical Cheshire landscape and these are most enjoyable, invariably passing through some of the attractive villages and by some of the county's outstanding churches or country houses. But you can also experience rough and challenging moorland hikes on the edge of the Peak District, plenty of attractive woodland walks along the sandstone ridge, or across parklands, or through the remnants of the medieval forests, a superb choice of peaceful canal walks and, on the Wirral, even coastal – or at least estuary – walking.

This book includes a list of waypoints alongside the description of the walk, so that you can enjoy the full benefits of gps should you wish to. For more information on using your gps, read the *Pathfinder® Guide GPS for Walkers,* by gps teacher and navigation trainer, Clive Thomas (ISBN 978-0-7117-4445-5). For essential information on map reading and basic navigation, read the *Pathfinder® Guide Map Reading Skills* by outdoor writer, Terry Marsh (ISBN 978-0-7117-4978-8). Both titles are available in bookshops or can be ordered online at www.totalwalking.co.uk

Wirswall Hill and Big Mere

		GPS waypoints
Start	Marbury, 3 miles north-east of Whitchurch (Shropshire)	⬛ SJ 561 457
Distance	3½ miles (5.6km)	**Ⓐ** SJ 556 458
Height gain	250 feet (75m)	**Ⓑ** SJ 553 456
Approximate time	2 hours	**Ⓒ** SJ 551 449
Parking	Roadside, with care, near village green and pub	**Ⓓ** SJ 550 444 **Ⓔ** SJ 548 441
Route terrain	Undulating, with one long gradual climb. Expect mud	**Ⓕ** SJ 553 439 **Ⓖ** SJ 556 444
Dog friendly	Lots of stiles; some may need dogs lifting over	
Ordnance Survey maps	Landranger 117 (Chester & Wrexham), Explorer 257 (Crewe & Nantwich)	

A pleasant stroll across fields and along a lane is followed by a short and easy climb up the slopes of Wirswall Hill, 495 ft (151m) high. Return along the well-waymarked South Cheshire Way. On the descent into Marbury, both the extensive vistas over the Cheshire plain and across Big Mere to Marbury Church are outstanding.

Marbury's 15th-century sandstone church occupies a superb site above Big Mere, the larger of the two meres around this peaceful and remote village.

⬛ The walk begins in the village centre by the green and **Swan Inn.** Turn along Wirswall Road; at steps and a stile opposite School Lane, take the waymarked stile, left, and head half-right to a stile by a gate. Climb this and keep ahead to a stile below a tree, then ahead again past low-spreading oaks to cross a footbridge **Ⓐ**.

Turn sharp left to use another stile and plank bridge and then trace the field road across a flat bridge, then a sleeper bridge. Look right for a stile by a concrete trough, use it and walk up the pasture to a stile onto a lane **Ⓑ**. Turn left and remain on this

Big Mere

winding lane for $^{1}/_{2}$ mile to reach a driveway on the left at the 'Wirswall' sign. Turn into this entry and use the stile on the right **C**.

Walk ahead up the hummocky field, take a stile beside a gate and continue in-line slightly left of the antenna on Wirswall Hill; pass by a waymarked old gatepost and rise to a stile onto the lane near the tall trees on the ridge **D**. Turn left and bend right with the lane, walking a further 400 yds to an open, fenced driveway on the left **E**. Turn along this, bend left with it, pass between farm buildings and, at a fork, keep right. Where this track bends left to a barn, go ahead through a stile and along the field edge to a fingerpost and stile **F**.

Turn left towards Marbury, shortly climbing a stile. Aim just left of the bushy hollow to find and use a waymarked gate. Head diagonally left down the pasture; near the bottom-left corner use two stiles in quick succession **G**. Walk ahead along the right-side of a field, climb a stile and veer slightly left through a shallow valley, passing an isolated waymarked tree, and continue across the uneven field, heading down to the left corner of woodland to reach a stile. Climb it and as you walk along the right edge of a field by woodland on the right, the views ahead of Big Mere and Marbury Church are particularly memorable.

Climb a stile in the field corner, keep ahead along a tree-lined path beside the mere, climb another stile and continue beside the mere. After climbing the next stile, turn right away from the water, head across the field to go through a gate onto a lane and turn left to the starting point of the walk. ●

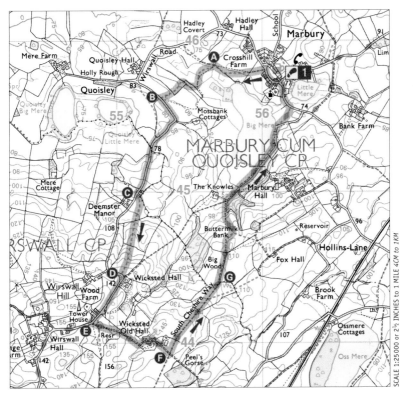

Bollington and Nab Head

		GPS waypoints
Start	Bollington	
Distance	3¾ miles (6km). Shorter version 2½ miles (4km)	☑ SJ 930 780
Height gain	670 feet (205m). Shorter version 280 feet (85m)	Ⓐ SJ 926 789
Approximate time	2 hours Shorter version 1½ hours	Ⓑ SJ 935 790
Parking	Middlewood Way car park, Adlington Road, Bollington (free)	Ⓒ SJ 937 784
Route terrain	Old railway, back lanes and field paths; steady climb to Nab Head	Ⓓ SJ 938 781
Ordnance Survey maps	Landranger 118 (Stoke-on-Trent & Macclesfield), Explorer 268 (Wilmslow, Macclesfield & Congleton)	Ⓔ SJ 940 788
		Ⓕ SJ 933 779

You begin by climbing steps onto a viaduct and the first part of the walk is along a disused railway track. Lanes, tracks and field paths lead to the base of Nab Head and this is followed by a short and relatively undemanding climb to the summit, 935 ft (285m) high and a magnificent viewpoint over the Cheshire plain. The shorter walk omits Nab Head and returns directly to Bollington.

With its stone houses, Victorian churches and chapels, mill buildings, aqueduct and railway viaduct, there is a real Pennine feel about Bollington.

☑ From the car park, take the fenced path beside the skateboard park and bend right with it, rising up a stepped ramp to gain the trackbed of an old railway. Walk away from the viaduct along this, once the Macclesfield to Marple Railway, now converted into the Middlewood Way, a multi-use recreational trail. At the second over-bridge (No. 8), leave the trail via the steps on your left, rising to a lane.

The Windmill pub is just to the left; the walk, however, turns right Ⓐ to cross the bridge and, shortly, a bridge over the Macclesfield Canal. Remain on the lane to a grassy triangular junction.

Turn left and at a public footpath sign, turn right over a stile, beside a Methodist church, and walk along an enclosed track to another stile. After climbing it, head uphill along the right edge of two fields, passing through a hedge gap, and climb a stile onto a lane Ⓑ.

Turn right along the lane and remain with it for about ½ mile to a slight right-hand bend Ⓒ. On the left here are a gate, gap stile and pond. Slip through the stile and head half-right to a stone stile. Continue along the right edge of the next field, go through a gate in the corner, descend steps to a track and turn right to a public footpath sign Ⓓ.

Keep ahead for the short walk, following route directions after the next way point Ⓓ appears in the text.

For the full walk, turn sharp left

along a walled track, descending steps, and continue in front of cottages down to a road. Turn left along Cocksheadhey Road and walk up it to a gateway. It is marked 'Private Road', but is a footpath, so use the hand-gate and go along the brick-paved drive. This narrows beside housing to a short, tarred path. Climb a stone stile, then a wooden stile and head slightly left, following the direction of low way-marked posts up across a sloping pasture.

Harrop Valley from Nab Head

Climb the stile in the top-left corner and bear left up the edge of the field to find redundant stone gateposts. Here turn right, tracing a path beside gorse to find the triangulation pillar on the summit of Nab Head **E**.

On clear days the views from here are spectacular and extensive, stretching across Macclesfield, Bollington and the Cheshire plain to Alderley Edge and the distant outline of Helsby Hill. The line of the Pennines and the hills of the Peak District can also be seen.

Retrace your steps to point **D** to rejoin the shorter walk and turn left

downhill along a walled tarmac track. On joining a lane, keep ahead steeply downhill, bending sharply to the left and continuing down to a road in Bollington. Turn right and, after going under the canal aqueduct, turn right into a park **F**. Turn left down steps, cross a footbridge over a stream and keep ahead beside it to join a tarmac path. Bear right, descend steps to recross the stream and the path bends left to continue through the park to a road opposite the car park. ●

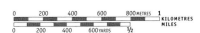

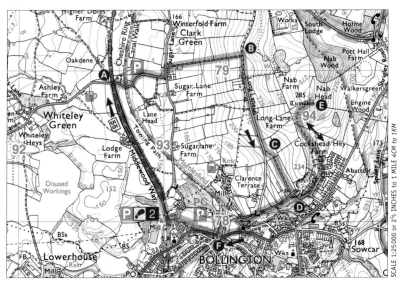

Little Budworth Country Park

		GPS waypoints
Start	Little Budworth Country Park about 3 miles west of Winsford	🥾 SJ 590 654
Distance	4 miles (6.4km)	**Ⓐ** SJ 586 652
Height gain	Negligible	**Ⓑ** SJ 579 660
		Ⓒ SJ 584 663
Approximate time	2 hours	**Ⓓ** SJ 590 664
Parking	Country Park car park (free)	**Ⓔ** SJ 595 661
Route terrain	Mostly sandy tracks, a few tarred lanes	**Ⓕ** SJ 599 656
Ordnance Survey maps	Landranger 117 (Chester & Wrexham), Explorer 267 (Northwich & Delamere Forest)	

The first half of this easy walk is through the attractive woodlands of Little Budworth Country Park. Later comes more open country and, towards the end, there is a memorable view of the tower of Little Budworth Church, rising above Budworth Pool. The whole area is congested and noisy when there is racing at Oulton Park (for race dates ring 01829 760301).

🥾 Turn left out of the car park *either along the road or cross over and take the parallel path through the trees* to a T-junction and turn right.

Pool and church at Little Budworth

Immediately bear left through the trees to pick up a path which keeps by the perimeter of Oulton Park racing circuit on the left. Cross a drive by the entrance to Oulton Park, keep ahead and the path emerges onto the main road near a

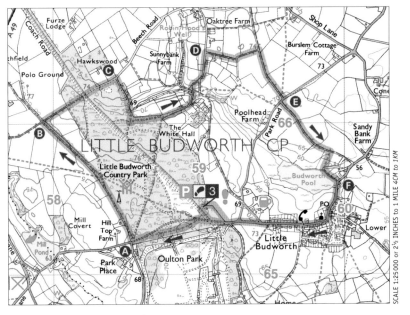

junction with Rushton Lane **A**.

Cross the main road to join the waymarked sandy lane, which skirts the left edge of woodland. Beyond the fields are the first wooded slopes of Delamere Forest. In just over ¹⁄₂ mile turn right at a cross-track **B**, joining another sandy lane, this time with Cheshire Polo Club's ground on your left. Cross straight over the minor road and keep ahead along Beech Road. At the far end of the woods turn right **C** along a track signed as a footpath for Whitehall Lane and Coach Road.

After passing to the right of a house, head down to climb a stile, keep to the left of a pool and the path continues through trees to a fork. Take the left-hand path and just beyond a purple arrow waymark, turn left onto a path which keeps parallel to the left edge of the wood. On emerging onto a track, continue along it, downhill, curving left in front of a house and passing to the right of a pond to reach a crossways. Keep ahead, curving right and heading gently uphill; just past a house called Minstead, and just after the track

becomes a tarred lane, turn right along a narrower tarred lane **D**.

Where this lane bends right, fork left along a hedge-lined track to a T-junction and turn right along another enclosed track to a road. Turn right; almost immediately turn left **E** onto a broad dirt track. As this splays into fields, keep ahead on the narrow, hedged path. In 300 yds take the waymarked stile on the right and walk straight across two horse pastures to a stile onto a path beside picturesque Budworth Pool. Turn left, enjoying views across to the village church in Little Budworth **F**.

Climb a stile onto a road, turn right and follow the road as it bends right through the village, passing between the **Red Lion** pub and the church. This is largely 18th century, apart from the 16th-century tower. Keep ahead and about 100 yds beyond the second road on the right (Park Road), bear right onto a path that winds back through woodland to the car park. ●

Styal and the Bollin Valley

Start	Styal, 1 mile north of Wilmslow	GPS waypoints
Distance	5 miles (8km)	🖉 SJ 835 835
Height gain	250 feet (75m)	Ⓐ SJ 833 833
		Ⓑ SJ 829 831
Approximate time	2½ hours	Ⓒ SJ 828 834
Parking	Village centre past The Ship Inn (free), Altrincham Road	Ⓓ SJ 816 829
		Ⓔ SJ 823 826
Route terrain	Dirt paths, byways, roads. Several lengthy flights of steps. Muddy in places	Ⓕ SJ 831 818
		Ⓖ SJ 839 821
Ordnance Survey maps	Landranger 109 (Manchester), Explorer 268 (Wilmslow, Macclesfield & Congleton)	

This walk visits the Bollin Valley, a stunning wooded gorge with a wealth of wildlife and specimen trees. Styal amply repays a walk around its cobbled lanes. The buildings were provided for his workers by Samuel Greg, an industrialist with a social conscience, way ahead of his time at the dawn of the Industrial Revolution. The remarkable Quarry Bank Mill and the old village are National Trust property.

🖉 From the rear of the car park turn left along the path and then right along the cobbled lane. Pass by the stump of a cross and join the enclosed path beside the lychgate to Norcliffe Chapel. Go straight across a track and enter the Northern Woods. Keep left at a fork to reach an information board Ⓐ.

Remain on the path in the trees, gradually descending through the superb woods above a deep little valley. Cross Kingfisher Bridge and follow a riverside path. After 200 yds go left at a fork, tracing the River Bollin to find Oxbow Bridge Ⓑ. Cross this and turn left along a wide path, shortly climbing a lengthy flight of stone steps. Cross a flat bridge before losing height again down more steps, at the foot of which keep ahead through a glade of huge beech trees. Climb a few steps and bend

right with the path to reach Giant's Castle Bridge Ⓒ.

Cross this and tackle another lengthy flight of steps, beyond which a fenced path skirts the boundary of woods and pasture. Descend steps and cross a wide footbridge, rejoining a riverside path. The woods here are excellent for wildflowers in spring and early summer; fungi in autumn. The path emerges from the trees as a wide, fenced way along the foot of sloping pastures. Re-enter the woods beside a tractor bridge (do not cross this), undulating through the woodland edge to reach a tarred lane Ⓓ.

Turn left and walk past the hotel. Cross the busy road at the bus stop and continue uphill. Turn right up railed steps to a kissing-gate. Head half-left, picking up a path beside trees on your

A chapel in Styal village

right. Slip through a gap and continue towards the houses, joining a raised embankment near a wooden pylon. Use a kissing-gate, turn left and trace the track to a lane **E**. Join the drive opposite for Chelsea Cottages. Walk in front of the cottages to a stile to the right-rear of a garage. Head just left of the tall trees in the field, climb a stile and continue ahead to use a stile into a lane; turn right. Opposite Moss Grove Farm, fork left along a hedged track. Go straight over a grassy cross-track; soon use a hand-gate and keep on a hedgeside path to reach a lane. Turn left to the main road **F**.

Cross straight over onto a gravel track, signed as a footpath to Twinnies Bridge and Kings Road. Keep ahead, eventually crossing a footbridge and rising to an estate road; turn left along this. Where this road bends sharp right, go ahead down the gated bridlepath, shortly crossing Twinnies Bridge **G**.

Turn left on a surfaced path left of the toilet block. At the far side of the green, use the long footbridge and take the first kissing-gate on the left, joining a wide sandy path beside the Bollin. At a T-junction turn left, walking above boggy woodland. Keep right at a fork and then ahead at junctions to reach Quarry Bank Mill. To return to Styal, walk up the tarred driveway and turn left at a sign for 'Styal Village'. Keep ahead on the sandy path, using several stiles/gates to return to the stump of the old cross. Turn right and then left to the car park. ●

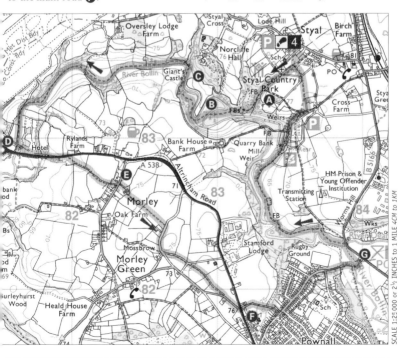

Dane Valley

		GPS waypoints
Start	Brereton Heath Country Park, off A54 between Congleton and Holmes Chapel	✏ SJ 795 653 Ⓐ SJ 795 657 Ⓑ SJ 800 671 Ⓒ SJ 810 671 Ⓓ SJ 809 676 Ⓔ SJ 799 675
Distance	5 miles (8km)	
Height gain	330 feet (100m)	
Approximate time	2½ hours	
Parking	Country Park (Pay & Display)	
Route terrain	Back lanes, tracks and field paths	
Ordnance Survey maps	Landranger 118 (Stoke-on-Trent & Macclesfield), Explorer 268 (Wilmslow, Macclesfield & Congleton)	

The route descends into the attractive valley of the meandering River Dane and continues on to the small and secluded village of Swettenham. After a circuit around the village, you retrace your steps to the start. The deep valley of Swettenham Brook is a good example of unimproved grassland. Next to the village pub is an interesting, compact arboretum.

Brereton Heath Country Park, an attractive area of grassland, woodland and lake, was created from a former sand quarry.

✏ Facing the lake, turn left and take the path to the left of the visitor centre. After 100 yds, just past a memorial bench, fork left on a grassy path, then sharp left to find a stile onto a lane, along which turn right.

At the main road Ⓐ, cross straight over and join the lane opposite – there are public bridleway and Dane Valley Way signs here – to a gate. Go through, continue along the drive to Davenport Hall and at a fork, take the right-hand drive which winds gently downhill into the lovely Dane valley. Go through a gate, cross a bridge over the River Dane and keep ahead along the track. After going through a gate, continue along a narrow lane which winds gently uphill into Swettenham. The church, a curious

but harmonious mixture of styles, dates from the Middle Ages but was mainly rebuilt in brick in the early 18th century.

At a public footpath sign opposite the church, turn right Ⓑ over a stile and walk along an enclosed path to another stile. Climb it, continue along the right edge of a field and at a fence corner, keep straight ahead, making for the corner with two waymarked lime trees, and then continue along the left field edge to a stile. Climb it, keep along the left edge of the next two fields, climbing more stiles, and where the fence and track bend left in the third field, keep straight ahead and climb a stile on the far side to emerge at a road junction. Take the second left Ⓒ, Congleton Road, wind down to cross Swettenham Brook and past two side roads. At a left bend, opposite the turn for Swettenham Heath, climb a stile on the left Ⓓ and walk ahead beside a

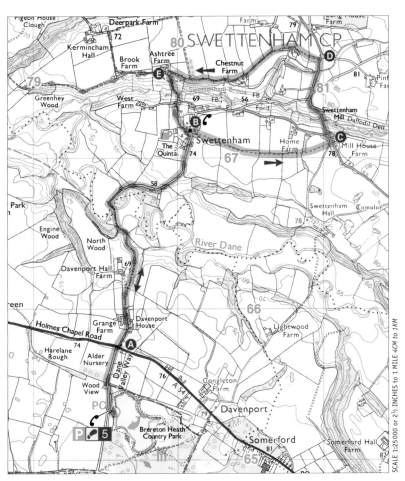

fence towards the house. After 150 yds swap sides via a stile and continue alongside the fence to a stile. Cross the drive and walk to the right of the barn to use another stile. Walk the left edge of two further pastures to find a stile into a lane; turn left along this peaceful old byway.

Not far past Chestnut Farm, a stile on the left allows access to Swettenham Meadows, a Cheshire Wildlife Trust Reserve conserving steep, unimproved grassland and wet-flush. It is an excellent area for insects, birds, wild flowers and shrubs; and walkways allow exploration. Return to the lane and turn left, walking through to the buildings at Ashtree Farm.

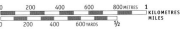

Turn sharp left at the waymarked gate **E** onto a steep, sunken woodland path that descends to cross a bridge over the brook before rising steeply to a T-junction. Turn right, then almost immediately left up a waymarked path that skirts the left side of a field. At the far side bear left, climb a stile and walk the grassy track to reach Swettenham Church. Bear right to a junction **B**. To view the specimen trees at the Quinta Arboretum, reach it via the garden beside the **Swettenham Arms** pub. To return to the start, turn right and reverse the outward route. ●

Chester and the River Dee

		GPS waypoints
Start	Chester	☑ SJ 405 662
Distance	5¼ miles (8.4km)	Ⓐ SJ 406 658
Height gain	165 feet (50m)	Ⓑ SJ 402 654
Approximate time	2½ hours	Ⓒ SJ 401 650
Parking	City centre car parks (Pay and Display/exit charge)	Ⓓ SJ 407 639
		Ⓔ SJ 409 645
Route terrain	Good paths, tracks and roads	Ⓕ SJ 410 640
		Ⓖ SJ 410 659
Ordnance Survey maps	Landranger 117 (Chester & Wrexham), Explorer 266 (Wirral & Chester)	Ⓗ SJ 407 661

This flat and easy walk to the south of Chester falls into two distinct halves. The first is through attractive woodland and across meadows bordering the River Dee. The second uses short stretches of Chester's medieval walls and passes some of the city's historic sites – allow plenty of time to explore one of England's most attractive, historic and fascinating cities.

Throughout its long history Chester has played many roles. Originally the Roman fort of Deva, it has been a major port (until the Dee silted up), both a defensive fortress against the Welsh and a springboard for English invasions of Wales, administrative centre and cathedral city.

Although none of the original gateways survive, Chester retains its circuit of medieval walls and most of its historic and architectural attractions lie within the walls. Foremost among these are the castle and cathedral. Of Chester's medieval castle, one of the principal fortresses along the Welsh border, only the 13th-century Agricola Tower remains. Most of it was pulled down in the late 18th and early 19th centuries and replaced by imposing classical buildings to serve as barracks and a law court. Chester Cathedral was originally a Benedictine abbey, raised to cathedral

status by Henry VIII in 1541 after the dissolution of the monasteries. The cloisters and other monastic buildings on the north side of the church are among its principal assets. Also worth seeing are the superb and intricately-carved 14th-century choir stalls, among the finest in the country. Most of the cathedral dates from the 14th and 15th centuries and it was heavily restored in the Victorian era.

Unique to Chester are the Rows, a series of covered walkways. These are medieval in origin, are found in the four main streets which radiate from The Cross and roughly correspond to the area originally enclosed by the Roman walls. Although their picturesque black-and-white appearance is more Victorian than Tudor, this in no way detracts from their appeal and attractiveness.

✎ From The Cross, walk down

Bridge Street and on down Lower Bridge Street, passing under Bridgegate to reach the Old Dee Bridge Ⓐ. Immediately turn right along Castle Drive and after passing County Hall, you can either continue along the road or take to the medieval walls, passing below the buildings of Chester Castle, to a main road. Cross over, turn left to cross Grosvenor Bridge and then bear right Ⓑ through a gap in the railings onto a path that drops parallel to the road into the strip of woodland. Turn left to pass under a footbridge and trace the path along the woodland floor to

Eastgate clock

the point where a crossing of paths is reached. Turn left and shortly climb steps up to railings beside a busy roundabout.

Your target is the ornamental gates diagonally opposite; carefully cross several roads to reach these. One is usually open, so walk ahead along the tarred track beyond. If closed, then walk 75 yds along Wrexham Road to railings and turn left Ⓒ on a tar path to reach the track, along which turn right. Remain on this, the Chester Approach to Eaton Hall, the Duke of Westminster's seat, for ¾ mile. Look on the left for a concrete ladder stile into a corner of pasture at the woodland edge. Do not use this, but instead take the path that runs beneath an overhanging yew tree just a few paces later Ⓓ, joining a path just within the left edge of the woods. Remain on this and keep left at a three-way junction of paths, keeping just within the woods. You'll reach a corner of the woods, at which point is a field gate and a track on your left. Fork right here, staying on a path through the woods which will deliver you to a deep pull-in beside a main road Ⓔ.

Cross to the pavement and turn right alongside Eaton Road. Follow this for 550 yds to reach a waymarked stile on the left (opposite an old cast iron sign for

Chester Cathedral

'City of Chester') **F**. Climb this into pasture and walk near to the field boundary on your left to a stile in the corner. Climb this and join a path that shortly passes by a pumping station before emerging from the trees as a way close to the bank of the River Dee. Remain with this through a series of old stiles and metal kissing-gates; the ample houses and boathouses of the suburb of Boughton eventually appearing on the opposite bank. The path becomes a gravel track beyond a kissing-gate. Remain on this around a left bend of the river, eventually reaching a final kissing-gate with an interpretation board explaining the 'Earls Eye' meadows you have just walked.

Keep ahead on the tarred track to reach the suspension footbridge over the Dee . Climb steps and cross this bridge, keep ahead up further steps before bending left around the edge of the grounds of the ruined St John's Church, which served briefly in the late 11th century as the cathedral of the Mercian diocese. Walk to the right of the Roman amphitheatre (dating from the 1st century AD) to reach Newgate, a reconstructed bridge on the line of the City walls. Immediately through the bridge, climb steps on the left up onto the walls, cross Newgate and walk through to Eastgate, topped by a distinctive clock tower, erected in 1897 to commemorate Queen Victoria's Diamond Jubilee. Look left from this to locate your starting point; use steps at either end of the bridge and head back to the Market Cross.

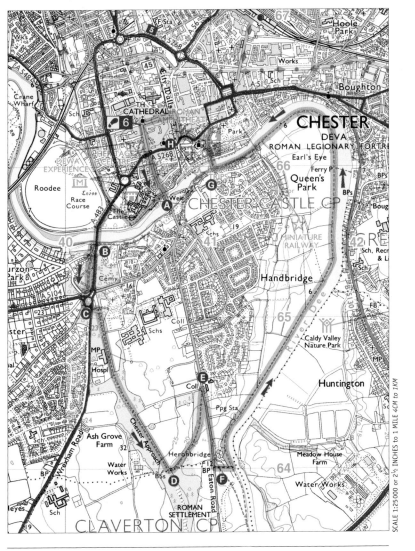

Boothsdale

		GPS waypoints
Start	Gresty's Waste car park, off A54 east of Kelsall	🥾 SJ 540 686
Distance	5¼ miles (8.4km)	Ⓐ SJ 539 692
		Ⓑ SJ 533 692
Height gain	690 feet (210m)	Ⓒ SJ 533 671
Approximate time	2½ hours	Ⓓ SJ 530 667
Parking	Sandstone Trail car park, Gresty's	Ⓔ SJ 534 661
	Waste (free)	Ⓕ SJ 539 672
Route terrain	Forestry roads, sandy paths and tracks, back lanes. Several steady climbs	Ⓖ SJ 539 678
Ordnance Survey maps	Landranger 117 (Chester & Wrexham), Explorer 267 (Northwich & Delamere Forest)	

This attractive walk is on the southern fringes of Delamere Forest and the first and last parts are through woodland. Most of the route is across open country and, from the higher points, there are fine and extensive views, especially looking towards the hills of North Wales on the horizon.

🥾 Pass to the right of the Sandstone Trail board and use the gap on the right onto the very busy A54. Carefully cross straight over and join the forestry road opposite, signed as the Sandstone Trail for Barnsbridge Gates and Forest Visitor Centre. Pass a barrier and walk gently uphill through the delightful Nettleford Wood.

In about ¹/₂ mile turn left Ⓐ at a fingerpost for Yeld Lane. The gravel forest track soon becomes a tarred lane past cottages; keep ahead at a junction and walk along Forest Gate Lane to a T-junction Ⓑ; here turn left. Descend the lane to a junction at the **Farmers Arms** pub. Cross straight over and walk along Waste Lane. At the end of the long straight, bend left at a chevron and then immediately turn right along a tarred driveway in front of a cottage. In just a few paces, drift right onto the greensward, walking a path through the

trees and signed for Willington. Go through a kissing-gate and keep ahead, walking the left edge of two pastures. The trees to your right shelter the site of an Iron Age hill fort. At a wooded corner climb a stile and drop down to join a path etched into the side of hidden Boothsdale. A lovely woodland-edge walk offers fine views down this wild flower-rich dale and across Cheshire to the Clwydian Mountains. The path merges with a gravel drive and just after this becomes tarred, turn sharp right Ⓒ along a narrow, hedged path. Keep ahead at the bottom end, shortly passing the rambler-friendly **Boot Inn**. Remain on this narrow lane to reach a T-junction; here cross the road and turn left along the pavement.

At a crossroads Ⓓ keep ahead on Willington Lane. It is a fairly quiet lane, but exercise care with oncoming traffic

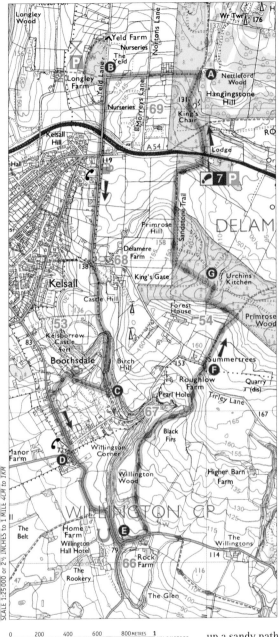

shaded lane to the edge of the woods. Turn left here, rejoining the Sandstone Trail at a fingerpost for Delamere Forest. A wide sandy track along the fringe of Willington Wood leads to a tarred lane. Turn left; in 50 paces fork right over a stile beside **Summertrees tearoom F**. The path skirts the tearoom and then traces a route via kissing-gates along the right edge of pastures. Look for a kissing-gate on your right and turn left through this, dropping to a further kissing-gate into Primrosehill Wood.

Go left along the wide path and keep right at the fork to reach a forestry road and interpretation board. Turn left, uphill to a nearby cross track **G**.

Keep ahead off the bend here in the direction of Delamere Forest and Frodsham, up a sandy path through immature woods. At the top, turn right and remain on this path through the edge of the woods, climbing several stiles before dropping into a sharp valley of mature pines. Cross a footbridge and climb the long flight of steps to return to the start. ●

(cross to the left just after a left-hand bend to tackle a very sharp right bend). Walk through to a junction opposite Willington Hall Hotel **E**. Turn left towards Utkinton and ascend the tree-

Astbury Mere and village

Start	Astbury Mere Country Park signed off the A34 just south of Congleton
Distance	5½ miles (8.8km)
Height gain	215 feet (65m)
Approximate time	2½ hours
Parking	County Park (free)
Route terrain	Good tracks and paths, towpath, pavement and field paths. May be muddy before Astbury
Ordnance Survey maps	Landranger 118 (Stoke-on-Trent & Macclesfield), Explorer 268 (Wilmslow, Macclesfield & Congleton)

GPS waypoints

- ✒ SJ 846 627
- Ⓐ SJ 851 623
- Ⓑ SJ 852 620
- Ⓒ SJ 864 620
- Ⓓ SJ 853 602
- Ⓔ SJ 849 605
- Ⓕ SJ 847 615
- Ⓖ SJ 845 619

From the shores of Astbury Mere on the outskirts of Congleton, the route proceeds mainly via enclosed tracks to the Macclesfield Canal. After a pleasant walk beside the canal, paths bring you to the attractive village of Astbury and, for much of the route, both tower and spire of its imposing church are in sight.

✒ Begin by taking the well-surfaced path which leads from the front of the visitor centre down to the lake and then bends left to continue beside it. At a fork by the corner of the lake, take the left hand uphill path, climb steps, keep ahead and turn right to climb more steps to a T-junction.

Turn right and the path bends left, becomes enclosed and continues above the mere before descending to a lane Ⓐ. Turn left and after about 400 yds, not far past Meadow Avenue, turn right along a waymarked path (if muddy, use the parallel track). The path merges with this tarred track anyway; when it does, continue along the track to reach the gates to a house Ⓑ.

Turn sharp left through a bridle-gate, signed as 'Lambert's Lane', towards Mossley. Remain on this sandy, hedged/fenced track, then cross a footbridge and bear left, rising gradually to pass

through a gate before walking past a remote house. On reaching the 'roving' bridge across the Macclesfield Canal, take the steps on the right Ⓒ down to the towpath and turn right. Remain on the towpath for 1¼ miles to reach Watery Lane Aqueduct Ⓓ. There is a stile on the right here, marked by a very low and worn stone post (it is also where the canal cuts through a line of tall trees). Use the stile, drop down to the lane and turn left, away from the narrow, damp tunnel beneath the canal. Follow the lane to reach a left bend Ⓔ.

Turn right over a fingerposted stile and keep ahead to cross a plank footbridge over a brook. Immediately bear left across a rather uneven field to a stile, climb it and walk along the right edge of the next field. Climb a stile, head across the field to climb a stile in the far right-hand corner and continue along the right edge of the next two fields. At a fence corner, turn right over a stile, bear right and head down across a field to climb another stile. Keep ahead across the next field – there are farm buildings to the left – and in the far left hand corner, climb a stile onto a road **F**. Turn left into Astbury.

With an imposing late medieval church and brick and half-timbered cottages grouped around a green, Astbury is a particularly attractive village. The sandstone church is one of the finest in Cheshire and has a curious design; the tower and spire stand at the north-west corner of the church and are almost detached from it. The interior is spacious and impressive, with a wide nave and some fine wood carving.

At a fork by the church bear right alongside the green to the main road

Boats on the Macclesfield Canal

and turn right, passing **The Egerton Arms** entrance. Turn right **G** along the lane called Fol Hollow, following this for ¹/₂ mile to reach a 30 mph restriction sign on the left **A**. Turn left along the footpath signed for Astbury Mere Country Park to reach the car park. ●

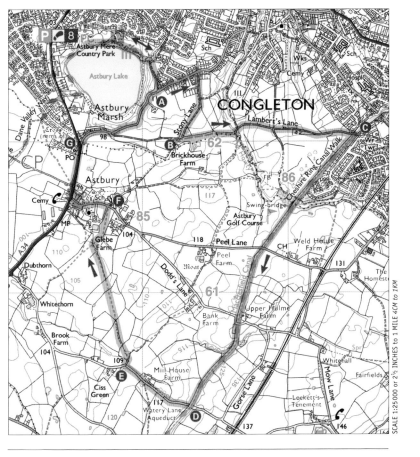

Delamere Forest

		GPS waypoints
Start	Linmere Lodge Forest Enterprise Visitor Centre	☑ SJ 548 704
Distance	5¾ miles (9.1km)	Ⓐ SJ 553 707
Height gain	410 feet (110m)	Ⓑ SJ 541 715
Approximate time	2½ hours	Ⓒ SJ 531 718
Parking	Large car park on site: Pay and Display	Ⓓ SJ 532 712
		Ⓔ SJ 539 704
Route terrain	Forestry tracks and paths; one steady, easy climb	Ⓕ SJ 543 697
Ordnance Survey maps	Landranger 117 (Chester & Wrexham), Explorer 267 (Northwich & Delamere Forest)	

Delamere Forest is a remnant fragment of the Norman hunting forest of Mara and Mondrum. Within this terrific mix of conifers and old broadleaves are hints of the netherworld; marshy, secluded 'schwingmoor' pools and stunning Blakemere, offering a primeval landscape enjoyed by ramblers, cyclists and horse riders. The walk includes Pale Heights, a magnificent viewpoint across the north west and into Wales.

☑ From the Visitor Centre, head for 'Go Ape' and railway station. Turn first left, over the bridge and then right along the wide path past the 'Go Ape' office and beneath its suspended wires and platforms to reach a junction beside Blakemere Ⓐ. Turn left along the wide track beside the mere, a striking lake formed over the past ten years in glacial kettle-holes originally drained 200 years ago to allow tree-growing for naval timber; gulls, wildfowl, newts and dragonflies thrive here. Remain with this track; keep right at Post 61 to reach another junction marked by benches and exercise stations. Here turn left onto the Delamere Way; trace this through to a wider forestry track and turn right, joining the Sandstone Trail (ST), presently reaching the main road at Barns Bridge Gates Ⓑ.

Cross this and go ahead on the forest road; in 100 yds turn left along the ST. The track strikes through to skirt the woodland edge; at a cross-track keep straight on, then bear left on the wider track, still the ST. At a major junction with low

The view from Pale Heights

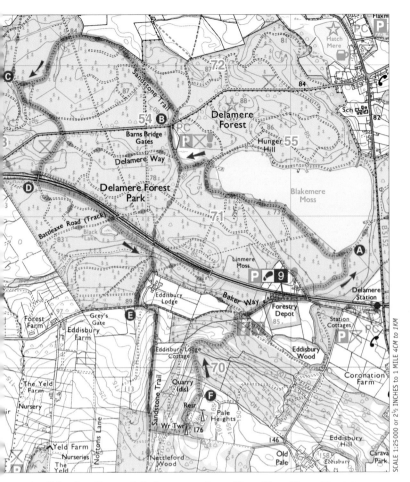

wood-rail fencing **C**, turn left along the Delamere Way (leaving ST) and carry on to the main road. Cross into the continuing forestry road; then fork right along the Delamere Loop bridlepath. Cross the bridge **D** and turn immediately left along the dirt path parallel to the railway cutting, threading beneath magnificent old hornbeams and oaks to reach the next bridge. Turn right, then within 20 paces drift left on a path to reach the Black Lake, a great picnic spot and famous for its dragon-flies (the logo of Delamere Forest).

Put the lake on your right and walk to its narrow end; bear left to a wider path and right on this, soon reaching a major junction of ways. Turn right along the wider, rising track; in 150 yds

keep right on the ST, climbing to a woodland edge roadway **E**.

Turn left; then right up the ST for Nettleford Wood. The track rises past a cottage to a gate and fingerpost; here turn left on the ST (alternative route) towards masts. Go straight over the wider track, then beside the young trees on your left to the monument on Pale Heights. On clear days the panorama is spectacular, with distant horizons of mountains, hills and estuary. Look for the 'Lancashire' standing stone and take the gravel path beside it **F**, dropping to the overflow car park where a right turn returns to the start. ●

Audlem and the Shropshire Union Canal

		GPS waypoints
Start	Audlem	
Distance	5¾ miles (9.2km)	
Height gain	130 feet (40m)	
Approximate time	2½ hours	
Parking	Audlem, Cheshire Street car park (free)	
Route terrain	Easy walking on field paths, tracks, towpath and byroads; muddy in places	
Ordnance Survey maps	Landranger 118 (Stoke-on-Trent & Macclesfield), Explorer 257 (Crewe & Nantwich)	

GPS waypoints

- ✐ SJ 659 436
- **A** SJ 662 436
- **B** SJ 665 443
- **C** SJ 666 449
- **D** SJ 669 459
- **E** SJ 663 462
- **F** SJ 656 465
- **G** SJ 648 465
- **H** SJ 658 435

This route is in the attractive valley of the River Weaver in south Cheshire. An opening stretch across fields is followed by a pleasant walk along the towpath of the Shropshire Union Canal. There are fine views throughout.

The Square in the centre of the attractive village of Audlem is dominated by the imposing, mainly 15th-century church. Below the church is the Shambles, a 17th-century buttermarket.

✐ Start in The Square and walk along Stafford Street, passing the church on your left. Pass by the turn into School Lane and bend right with the main road. Opposite the other end of School Lane, turn left **A** along a lane and where it bends left after 150 yds, fork ahead-right along Mill Lane. As this turns left to cottages, keep ahead on the hedged path (a muddy bridleway), eventually joining a lane. Turn left and walk to a sharp left bend; here turn right **B**, along the tarmac drive to The Parkes. Just before reaching gateposts, bear left to climb a stile, walk along the left edge of a field and go through a kissing-gate onto a road.

Turn left **C** then almost immediately turn right up steps (which may be overgrown) to use a stile. Walk the right-hand field edge. At the first corner climb the gate-side stile and trace the right edge of the next field to the corner. Turn left and after 20 paces use the waymarked gate on the right and walk ahead through the rubble-strewn yard, passing left of the barn to reach a lane. Go ahead along this; as it ends at gates and a cattle-grid take the path on the left **D**.

This is waymarked as the South Cheshire Way (SCW). Walk along the left edge of a field, climb a stile, keep ahead along an enclosed path and after climbing the next stile, the route continues along the right edge of a field. Head gently downhill along a track which curves right and, immediately after crossing a tractor bridge over the River Weaver **E**, turn left along the riverbank to a stile. Climb this and rise uphill to use another stile. Follow the left edge of this very long field to a further stile, climb this and head half-right to find an old waymarked gate not far from the far-right corner **F**.

After going through it, bear left along the left edge of a field to a stile, climb it and keep ahead by a line of trees on the left which indicate the line of a former field boundary. Go through a hedge gap beside a redundant stile, continue along the right edge of the next field, climb a stile onto a lane and turn left. At a public footpath sign, turn right along a track and, in front of a canal bridge, turn right through a gate and descend to the tow-path of the Shropshire Union Canal **G**.

Turn sharp left, pass under the bridge and keep by the canal for 2 miles back to Audlem. On approaching a pub called the **Shroppie Fly**, bear left off the towpath to emerge onto a road by the **Bridge Inn** **H** and turn left to return to The Square.

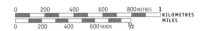

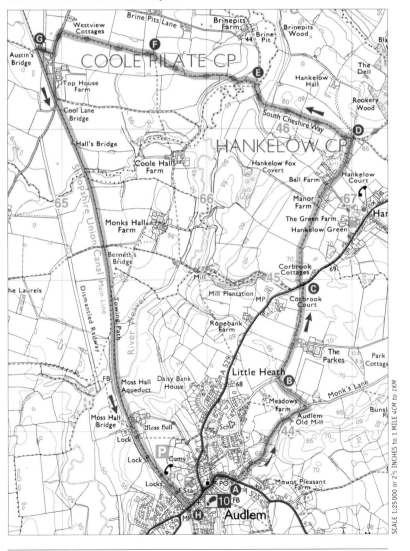

SCALE 1:25000 or 2½ INCHES to 1 MILE 4CM to 1KM

Bulkeley Hill and Raw Head

		GPS waypoints
Start	Bickerton Poacher pub, Bulkeley, on A534	🖉 SJ 523 544
		Ⓐ SJ 523 549
Distance	5¾ miles (9.3km)	Ⓑ SJ 526 552
Height gain	935 feet (285m)	Ⓒ SJ 526 558
Approximate time	3 hours	Ⓓ SJ 522 564
Parking	Sandstone Trail car park at the pub (free)	Ⓔ SJ 515 562
		Ⓕ SJ 518 551
Route terrain	Woodland and field paths, lanes, several modest climbs; sheer drops at Ⓑ and Ⓖ	Ⓖ SJ 508 548
		Ⓗ SJ 514 540
Ordnance Survey maps	Landranger 117 (Chester & Wrexham), Explorer 257 (Crewe & Nantwich)	

Much of the route is along the well-wooded sandstone ridge that runs across Cheshire. After climbing Bulkeley Hill, you continue to Raw Head, the highest point on the ridge. The whole walk provides a succession of superb viewpoints from relatively modest heights and for relatively little effort as most of the climbing is steady rather than strenuous.

🖉 Stand with your back to the Sandstone Trail board in the car park and carefully cross the main road to the steps and kissing-gate. Walk up the enclosed path and just as it enters woodland, turn right through a fence-gap and walk the waymarked path up through the trees. Go up steps, through a kissing-gate, then up more steps before turning right at a path T-junction, soon skirting the right-edge of a rough meadow. Re-enter the woods via a kissing-gate and turn left. In 30 paces, fork slightly right to reach a glade beneath tall pines Ⓐ. Join the Sandstone Trail here, turn right and tackle a short, steep climb to the highest levels of Bulkeley Hill. Pass into National Trust woods. In places, rocky outcrops allow extensive views east across Cheshire to the Peak District's hills.

Simply stick to the main path close to the lip of the extremely steep slope Ⓑ.

The path reaches a beautiful glade of particularly gnarled chestnut trees. On your right, two concrete blocks mark the top of a tramway erected when reservoirs were being built – look over the edge to view the steep incline here. Remain with the Sandstone Trail, still following the edge for a while before gradually veering into the woods, shortly dropping down a flight of rough steps to reach a T-junction. Turn right along the sandy track, from which are the first glimpses of the sweeping views west to the Clwydian Mountains, to reach a lane in front of an ornate gatehouse to the Peckforton Estate Ⓒ.

Turn left and after 20 paces look right for a Sandstone Trail fingerpost and kissing-gate. This is the first of a series

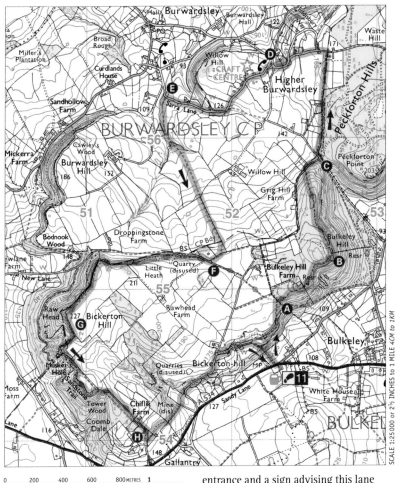

SCALE 1:25000 or 2½ INCHES to 1 MILE 4CM to 1KM

of such gates, taking the path along the top of pastures and enclosed wood-side sections to eventually emerge onto a tarred lane. Turn left towards Pheasant Inn and Beeston and leave the Sandstone Trail. Keep ahead at the junctions to reach a cross-lanes **D**. To reach the **Pheasant Inn** turn right, then right again for about 200 yds; otherwise go straight across and bend left with the lane, reaching a junction within 50 yds. Turn left, immediately passing by the lower entrance to the Cheshire Workshops. The lane shortly passes the upper

entrance and a sign advising this lane as 'unsuitable for motor vehicles'.

Remain on the lane past a cottage; bend right (ignore the waymarked path left) and drop gently through a secluded valley past more cottages. At the next sharp-right bend, take the fingerposted stile on the left **E**, walking a path parallel to a fence on your right, marking the edge of a marshy watercourse. This direction brings you to a wooded corner and a gated footbridge. Cross this and cut up the path through the dell, emerging over a stile into rising pasture. Pass left of the trees in the middle of the field to a stile, climbing then to a kissing-gate into a roughly surfaced track. Go straight across, over a stile and up the edge of this long field, eventually finding a stile in the top corner. Turn right beside the fence, passing through the stand of birch to gain a rough lane .

Turn right along the Sandstone Trail. After 75 yds fork right on a tree-lined path. After a further 75 yds fork left to and through a kissing-gate. At a fork keep ahead on the Sandstone Trail, shortly climbing a gradual flight of steps. Looking back, the edifices of Beeston and Peckforton castles may be seen protruding from the northern end of the sandstone ridge. Pass by a rocky viewpoint. Ignore steps down to the right and remain on the woodland-edge Sandstone Trail, eventually gaining the triangulation pillar on Raw Head. Take time to digest the huge views from this modest hilltop, just 745ft (227m) above sea level **G**.

Depart along the Sandstone Trail, shortly arriving at a long and potentially slippery flight of rough stone steps. Keep left on the Sandstone Trail at a junction, the path rising and falling over a series of little headlands within the woods. Eventually, the path leaves the woods, becoming a wide, fenced path leading to a kissing-gate into a rough lane beside Chiflik Farm. Walk down this to a right-hand bend **H**.

Fork left on a dirt path and then turn left at the fingerpost for 'Coppermine Lane'. Trace the enclosed path to and across a footbridge, rising then by a fence, left, to reach a corner stile. The chimney in the pasture here is one of the few visible remains of the little-known, long-gone copper mining industry in Cheshire. Turn left up Coppermine Lane and then after about 350 yds, turn right along a rough driveway, forking immediately left. At the end of this track climb a stile into woodland, sticking close to the wall/fence on your right. Use a hand-gate, descend steps and shortly join the path back to the nearby pub. ●

Bulkeley Hill

Sandbach

		GPS waypoints
Start	Sandbach Market Square	🖊 SJ 758 608
Distance	6 miles (9.7km)	Ⓐ SJ 761 606
Height gain	165 feet (50m)	Ⓑ SJ 760 601
Approximate time	3 hours	Ⓒ SJ 780 586
Parking	Sandbach (Pay & Display)	Ⓓ SJ 750 592
Route terrain	Field paths, towpaths, back lanes	Ⓔ SJ 753 598
Ordnance Survey maps	Landranger 118 (Stoke-on-Trent & Macclesfield), Explorer 268 (Wilmslow, Macclesfield & Congleton)	Ⓕ SJ 754 602

You escape from the bustle of Sandbach into a secluded valley. After a noisier stretch close to the M6, most of the return leg is peaceful, first beside the Trent and Mersey Canal between Hassall Green and Wheelock, and finally through another secluded valley on the edge of the town.

🖊 The walk starts in the town centre by the Sandbach Crosses, a pair of carved 9th-century Anglo-Saxon crosses. Walk towards the war memorial and turn left down High Street, passing to the right of the large and handsome church, built mainly in 1633 and restored in the Victorian era.

At the A534 traffic lights Ⓐ, cross over and turn right alongside it. Cross the end of Palmer Road and then fork left along a grassy hollow. At the brook, turn left and walk through to the foot of an earth bank, just a few paces before reaching houses. Turn right here along an overgrown path to find a stile next to a field-gate. Climb this and turn left up the field edge. Use another stile in the top corner and walk ahead along the access lane to a junction Ⓑ.

Turn left, turn right at a T-junction and at a public footpath sign, turn left along an enclosed track. Where the track curves right at a waymarked post, bear left onto a path by the left edge of

a field and at a hedge corner, the path veers slightly right, continues downhill and descends steps to cross a footbridge over a brook. Continue uphill along the right edge of a field, go through a kissing-gate, keep ahead to go through another, cross a track and go through another kissing-gate. Turn right along a path, cutting diagonally across a field, aiming to arrive at a stile at the corner of fencing just to the left of an imposing house. Climb this and bend left with the path as it drops into a wooded dell to reach a stile beside a bridge.

Cross the track and use the kissing-gate opposite, joining a path above a brook. Pass a derelict stile and then keep an eye out for the waymarked footbridge on your right. Cross this and head half-left on a path diagonally up the bank. Pass by the row of three in-field oaks and then swing half-right to a stile through the distant fence. Climb this and walk ahead, parallel to the M6, to two adjoining stiles into a lane.

Turn left, cross the motorway bridge and then look for a stile on the right; here double-back along a fenced path, climb a further stile and then walk the field edge near the top of the motorway embankment. The boundary bears away from the M6; simply remain on the field edge path to find a stile through a tall hedge. Walk the enclosed path and keep ahead along the cul-de-sac. Cross diagonally over the green and walk the road to a T-junction **C**. Turn right; pass right of the **Romping Donkey** pub and cross the canal bridge.

Turn right onto the towpath, water on your right, pass under the motorway and keep beside the canal for about 1¾ miles to Wheelock. Just before reaching bridge 154, bear left up to a road **D**. Turn right to cross the bridge, immediately turn right down steps, at a public footpath sign to Mill Hill Lane and walk ahead beside the canal as far as a waymarked post where the canal narrows. Turn left here onto a path through woodland, turn right to cross a footbridge over a brook and turn left alongside it, passing under a former railway bridge.

0	200	400	600	800 METRES	1
0	200	400	600 YARDS	½	KILOMETRES MILES

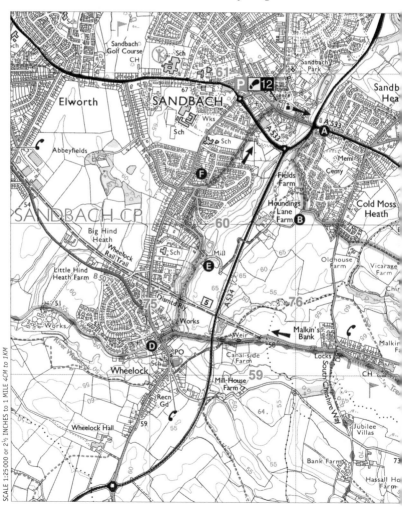

SCALE 1:25000 or 2½ INCHES to 1 MILE 4CM to 1KM

Sandbach town centre

Climb a stile and keep ahead on the path, cross two footbridges and then trace the path across the foot of a sloping field. Bear left to cross a brook and the path then bears right and winds through trees to a narrow lane at an old mill **E**. Turn left and go uphill past housing. Shortly after passing Mill Hill Drive on your right, turn right along a waymarked, enclosed path, which bends right to emerge onto a road. Turn left, turn left again at a T-junction, turn right at the next T-junction and turn right again at another T-junction.

Take the first road on the left (Price Avenue) and then almost immediately bear right along an enclosed track (Price Drive) **F**. Now keep ahead, walking in a straight line which leads you along a series of tracks and paths – crossing several roads (including a main road near a Waitrose) – to return directly to the start. ●

Disley and Lyme Park

Start	Disley station	GPS waypoints
Distance	6 miles (9.6km)	⬛ SJ 972 845
Height gain	935 feet (285m)	Ⓐ SJ 973 844
		Ⓑ SJ 981 831
Approximate time	3 hours	Ⓒ SJ 976 830
Parking	Disley station car park (free)	Ⓓ SJ 981 822
		Ⓔ SJ 973 812
Route terrain	Tracks, lanes and fields. One long steady climb, several short ones	Ⓕ SJ 964 824
		Ⓖ SJ 966 841
Dog friendly	Dogs on leads in Lyme Park (points Ⓔ – Ⓖ)	
Ordnance Survey maps	Landranger 109 (Manchester), Explorer OL1 (The Peak District – Dark Peak area)	

This highly scenic walk follows the first part of the Gritstone Trail along an old routeway into Lyme Park. Then comes a short circuit of the park before returning to Disley. The superb views range from the built-up area of Greater Manchester to the bare moorlands of the Peak District and the route passes Lyme Hall, well worth a visit. Note that the parkland gate at Ⓖ is locked at 18.00

⬛ Find the Gritstone Trail information board near the station building. Climb the flight of steps here, keeping left at a split and rising through woods to a lane. Go ahead uphill and in a short distance fork left Ⓐ towards St Mary's Church and then bend right with this lane, which soon roughens to a walled track, Green Lane. There are fine views all round, including The Cage, a 16th-century tower built as a viewing platform for the hunt. Keep ahead at Higher Stoneridge Farm, the track narrowing to a path before reaching a stile. Climb this and continue ahead, fording a shallow brook and then rising to a gate and crossways Ⓑ.

Go right down the rough lane, cross a bridge and rise to use a stile on your left, signed for Bowstones Ⓒ. Aim just left of the nearest pylon; beyond this a

waymarked post (Gritstone Trail Alternative Route) indicates the way. A series of these take you above trees before, 50 yds past a gateway, dropping left to a stile and gate in a dingle 100 yds below a ruinous barn. Use the nearby kissing-gate and turn right, climbing a reedy path beside a wall, presently reaching the farm on the hillside ahead. Look for the waymarked handgate into the yard (just left of the right-hand barn), walk through and follow the driveway to a road junction Ⓓ.

Turn sharp right up the lane for Dissop Head Farm, commencing a steady, easy climb around the flank of Higher Moor. Magnificent views open out across Whaley Moor to the long line of distant Brown Knoll and the plateau of Kinder Scout, highest point in the Peak District. The lane winds to reach a

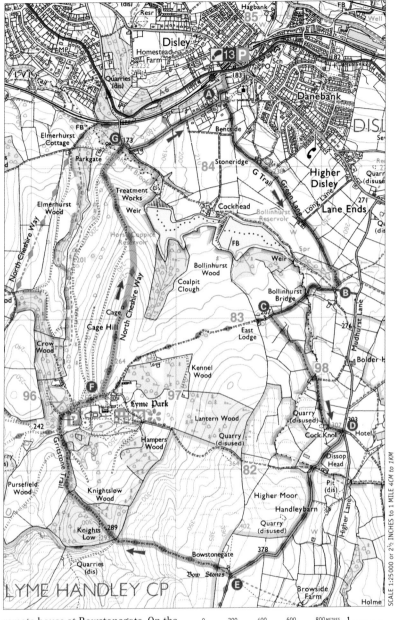

SCALE 1:25000 or 2½ INCHES to 1 MILE 4CM to 1KM

remote house at Bowstonegate. On the right here, a small fenced enclosure surrounds the Bowstones, the weathered stumps of Saxon crosses that mark an ancient boundary. Views stretch ahead to shapely Shutlingsloe and, left of this, the ridge up to Shining Tor, Cheshire's highest point (1,834 feet/559m).

Use the stile (Gritstone Trail) **E** at the near end of the drive and go ahead to another nearby. Join the braided path dropping steeply across Park Moor to reach a woodland-edge gate. Enter Knightslow Wood and trace the wide path ahead to the far side of the trees;

The Cage, Lyme Park

there is an excellent viewpoint to Lyme Hall from this woodland path. Leave the woods and bear right, dropping beside the fallow deer enclosure wall to a tight kissing-gate beside a parkland gate. Go through and turn right across the car park to find the NT Information Centre. Climb the irregular flight of stone steps left of this to reach the main entrance to Lyme Hall.

Lyme Hall belonged to the Legh family for nearly 600 years until Richard Legh, third Lord Newton, gave the Estate to the National Trust in 1946. This north front is part of the original 16th century mansion built for Sir Piers Legh, as are the drawing room and long gallery. Over the next 300 years the house was enlarged and rebuilt several times, notably in the early 18th century by the Italian architect Leoni and again a century later by Lewis Wyatt. Leoni's main contribution was the classical south front, the most imposing view of the Hall (visible from the Gardens, fee payable – the famous BBC *Pride and Prejudice* lake is here, too). The Hall is noted for its Mortlake tapestries, furniture, Grinling Gibbons woodcarving and English clocks.

F Put your back to the gateway and walk half-right, up the steeper drive bending right. Cut ahead off this bend on the higher path along the low ridge, walking through to the distinctive building on the ridge-crest ahead. This is The Cage, built as a hunting lodge by the Leghs and also used as a prison for poachers who targeted Lyme Park's herds of both red and fallow deer, still present in large numbers today. Carry on straight past it on a stony track that meets the main driveway. Turn right to the wooden pay-lodge **G**.

Fork right to the gate beside Red Lane Lodge and walk the rough lane beyond past imposing houses to reach **A**. Turn left and drop to the corner, from here take the path back down to Disley Station.

Dunham Park and the Bridgewater Canal

		GPS waypoints
Start	Oldfield Brow, about 1 mile north west of Altrincham	SJ 751 888
Distance	6½ miles (10.5km)	Ⓐ SJ 726 885
Height gain	Negligible	Ⓑ SJ 722 874
Approximate time	3 hours	Ⓒ SJ 735 873
Parking	Seamons Road Trans Pennine Trail car park (free)	Ⓓ SJ 745 874 Ⓔ SJ 742 878
Route terrain	Easy walking on lanes, field paths, old railway and towpath	Ⓕ SJ 739 882
Dog friendly	Several high ladder stiles; dogs on leads in Dunham Park	
Ordnance Survey maps	Landranger 109 (Manchester), Explorers 268 (Wilmslow, Macclesfield & Congleton) and 276 (Bolton, Wigan & Warrington)	

This route makes use of a disused railway track on the outward leg and the towpath of the Bridgewater Canal on the final stretch. In-between you walk through part of the park surrounding the great house of Dunham Massey. There are wide views across the pleasant countryside of the Bollin valley which lies between the Greater Manchester and Merseyside conurbations.

Start by turning left along a straight track, once a railway line between Altrincham and Warrington and now part of the Trans-Pennine Trail. Keep along it for 1½ miles, passing under one bridge, to emerge onto a road (Station Road) Ⓐ.

Turn left into Dunham Woodhouses and just after the road bends left in the village centre, turn right along an enclosed track (Meadow Lane). After crossing a bridge over the River Bollin, keep ahead over a stile and veer slightly left across a field to cross a footbridge over a brook. Bear slightly right and head uphill across a field, climb a stile on the brow and keep ahead across the

next field to a fingerpost attached to a wooden pylon Ⓑ. Turn left to a stile at the nearby offset field corner.

Use this stile and put the hedge on your right, walking through to another stile at the edge of woodland. Climb this and keep ahead across rough pasture towards the housing beyond the distant pylon. Climb another stile to join a sunken lane, remaining on this beneath the aqueduct carrying the Bridgewater Canal. The track rises to a triangular green in Little Bollington. Turn left past the **Swan with Two Nicks** pub, shortly after which cross the footbridge over the Bollin. Continue along a tarmac track and where it bends left, pass beside a gate and walk along a straight, fence-lined path towards the buildings of Dunham Massey.

Climb a ladder stile to enter Dunham Park and keep ahead along a tarmac drive to a fork in front of the Hall **C**. Dunham Massey Hall was built for the Earl of Warrington in the 18th century and remodelled in the early 20th century. It is noted for the richness of the interior and the fine collections of furniture, silver and paintings. There are colourful gardens and the surrounding deer park, laid out in the early 18th century, has some impressive avenues.

At the fork, take the right-hand drive and continue across the deer park, curving left to a lodge. Climb a ladder stile onto a road, **D** turn left and take the first lane on the right. At a footpath fingerpost take the kissing-gate on the right and follow the wide path ahead across the field to a waymarked post, here turn left along the right-hand side of the field. Climb a stile onto a lane, turn right and at a public footpath sign, turn left over a stile and walk across a field to a waymarked post on the far side. Turn left **E** along an enclosed path, pass beside a fence and continue to a road in Dunham Town which, despite its name, is only a hamlet.

Turn right along School Lane, shortly passing by the **Axe & Cleaver** pub. Remain on the lane to cross the canal bridge **F**, turn sharp right down a path and through a kissing-gate onto the towpath of the

Dunham Massey Sawmill

Bridgewater Canal. Turn left and keep beside the canal for 1 mile to Seamons

Fallow deer in Dunham Park

Moss Bridge. Just before reaching it, turn left up steps to a road and turn left to return to the start. ●

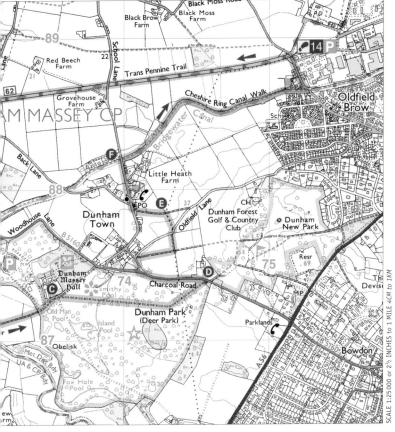

Wybunbury

Start	Wybunbury, 2 miles south east of Nantwich	GPS waypoints
Distance	6¼ miles (10km)	⬈ SJ 699 498
Height gain	310 feet (95m)	Ⓐ SJ 689 485
Approximate time	3 hours	Ⓑ SJ 697 471
Parking	Roadside near old church tower	Ⓒ SJ 704 482
Route terrain	Lanes and field paths, muddy in places	Ⓓ SJ 714 490
		Ⓔ SJ 713 502
Dog friendly	Lots of stiles, some very awkward for dogs	Ⓕ SJ 705 506
Ordnance Survey maps	Landranger 118 (Stoke-on-Trent & Macclesfield), Explorer 257 (Crewe & Nantwich)	

From the hilltop village of Wybunbury, the route follows paths across the undulating country of south Cheshire. Towards the end it passes the edge of Wybunbury Moss, a National Nature Reserve. For much of the way, Wybunbury's imposing church tower is in sight.

The tall, 15th-century church tower at Wybunbury stands on its own; unstable ground caused the church to be rebuilt several times throughout its history and it was finally abandoned and demolished in the 1970s. A modern church building is nearby.

⬈ The walk starts by the **Swan Inn**. Facing the church tower, walk down the hill to the right of it and just after crossing a bridge over Wybunbury Brook, turn right, at a public footpath sign, along a tarmac track. Cross a cattle-grid and turn left up the field edge, climbing a stile up steps in the first corner. Turn right to use another stile in the nearby corner; then trace the left-edge of this huge field, joining a field road that leads to the A51.

Turn right and after 75 yds use the stile on the left and walk ahead, passing left of the high cupressus hedge. As the fence turns away drift right to use stiles

and a footbridge in the corner. Go ahead, looking for a stile beneath an oak as the fence curls right; once over which turn right. Where the boundary turns right, keep straight on to a stile at the far side.

Drop slightly right beneath cables into the overgrown valley, cross another footbridge/stile combination and climb ahead via a string of stiles to gain a tarred farm road Ⓐ. Turn left along this; as it bends left, turn right at a stile by a lone tree and walk to a stile in the hedgerow ahead. Use this and keep ahead to a stile beside a gate. Turn left along the rough lane here – there's a fishing pool on your left – and follow the track around a number of bends to a road. **Dagfields Craft Centre** (which has cafés) is to the left; the route continues to the right. Take the first lane on the left (Lodge Lane) and follow it around a right bend to a T-junction. Turn left and

after ¼ mile, turn left, at a waymarked stile opposite the gates to a house named 'Hunsterson House', here joining the South Cheshire Way **B**.

Walk along the right-hand field edge and then trace the path to the left around the sinuous edge of Birchenhill Wood, to find a waymarked footbridge on your right 75 yds past a distinct

corner. Cross this and rise through the copse-edge to a gate-side stile. Keep ahead to use another stile at the far end of a garden wall. Walk to the stile opposite and turn left on the track to reach the busy A51.

Turn left; cross where safe and take the turn for Jacobs View Lake **C**. This roughening lane drops gradually to cross a bridge. Continue uphill to a waymarked bridleway beneath a mobile phone mast. Immediately past a bridlegate, look right for a stile high in the hedgerow; use this and turn left along the field edge. Remain with this boundary via redundant stiles to find a kissing-gate into pasture to the left of converted barns. Another kissing-gate below poplars leads onto a driveway through to a lane **D**.

Turn left and after 75 yds use the waymarked field gate on the right. Head slightly left, cresting a brow and dropping to a stile in a boggy hollow. Climb it and turn right to find and use another in an overgrown corner; then turn left up the field edge to reach stiles at a concrete farm lane. Cross straight over and walk to and past the second in-field telegraph pole, continuing in the same line past a reedy pond to an offset field corner. Put a hedge on your right and remain with the field edge path to reach the rear of houses. Look right for a stile, then turn left over another and walk beside the house to a lane **E**.

Use the kissing-gate opposite and trace the right edge to another. Walk half-left, round the right-hand hedge corner and through a further kissing-gate to the right of silage clamps. Two more such gates find you at the left edge of a spinney. Continue to a nearby third gate, on your right **F**. Do not use this; rather, head half-left, passing right of the nearest electricity pylon to find a fenced corner with a pond on your right.

Skirt the pond, climb a stile and cut half-left across the horse-pasture to another stile. Drop to the foot of the paddock and a further stile. Now look ahead for a stile through rail fencing: beyond this drop gently to another beneath a tall oak. Here join the path ahead along the fringe of Wybunbury Moss, a National Nature Reserve protecting a very rare floating bog, a thick crust of peat covering a lake 40 feet (12m) deep. Beyond some boardwalk, a flat bridge and gate, walk ahead towards the church tower. The path scurries up the bank to a kissing-gate leading into the churchyard and a return to the adjacent Swan Inn.

Pond near Wybunbury

Farndon and Churton

		GPS waypoints
Start	Farndon	📷 SJ 412 543
Distance	6¼ miles (10km)	Ⓐ SJ 415 548
Height gain	115 feet (35m)	Ⓑ SJ 429 550
Approximate time	3 hours	Ⓒ SJ 424 566
Parking	Picnic area beside the Dee bridge (free)	Ⓓ SJ 417 564
		Ⓔ SJ 400 556
Route terrain	Field paths and byways; riverside path can be muddy	
Ordnance Survey maps	Landranger 117 (Chester & Wrexham), Explorer 257 (Crewe & Nantwich)	

A pleasant walk across fields leads to Churton and from there the route continues through woodland to the River Dee. The remainder of the route is mostly beside the winding river. The wide views across the surrounding terrain extend from Cheshire's sandstone ridge to the Clwydian hills of North Wales.

Farndon is an attractive village of stone and black-and-white, half-timbered cottages. The church, of medieval origin, was mainly rebuilt in the 17th century after being damaged in the Civil War.

📷 Start at the picnic area by the 14th-century bridge over the River Dee and walk along a track away from the bridge. Just before reaching a boardwalk, bear left along a path which curves left and climb steps through woodland. At the top, turn right and then left along a hedged track (shortly a tarred driveway), then turn right at the end to reach the main road.

Cross straight over into Walkers Lane, go through a kissing-gate and continue along the left edge of a field. Go through a kissing-

gate, keep ahead across the next field and at a footpath post by a hedge corner, turn right Ⓐ and continue along the left field edge. At another hedge corner, keep straight ahead across the field and climb a stile onto a road. Turn left and at a public footpath sign to Churton and Coddington, turn right

Cheshire countryside near Farndon

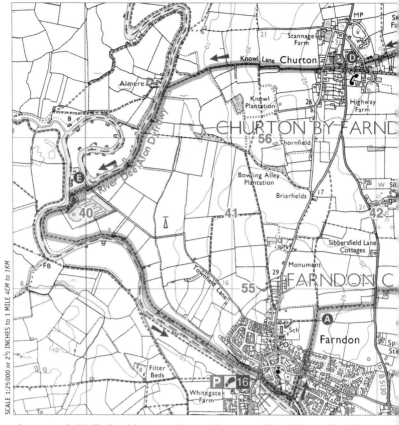

along a track. Walk ahead between the barns and ahead left along the concrete track. Where this track ends, go through the gate and head diagonally left across the pasture to the far corner. Here cross a plank bridge and a stile, walk along

Bridge over River Dee at Farndon

field, climb a stile and continue along a tarmac track to a T-junction in the pleasant village of Churton. Turn left, at the next T-junction turn right to a road, turn right and almost immediately turn left beside the **White Horse** pub along Hob Lane **D**. Where the lane bends left, keep ahead along a rough track, Knowl Lane. Go round one zigzag; at a second one ignore the path signed left for Farndon, walk on a few more paces and then turn left along a hedged green lane, remaining with this through a kissing-gate before walking through a belt of woodland. At the far end turn left along the riverside path beside the River Dee.

At the wood's end go through a kissing-gate and remain with the waterside path, soon reaching the first of many secluded, occasionally eccentric chalets and cabins which pepper both banks of the Dee for the rest of the walk. Passing left of the chalet, continue along to a kissing-gate immediately above a sharp bend in the river and walk through to the rough lane **E**.

Go through the kissing-gate opposite and walk the left edge of the pasture to use two hand-gates. Keep ahead to a crossways amid chalets and here turn right, putting some ponds on your left. Immediately after the last chalet, turn right along a narrow, fenced path, use the kissing-gate beside a huge crack willow tree and join a riverside path. Remain on this, pass along a path (bordered by a high security fence on the left) to the right of another chalet and then continue beside the riverside trees. At a kissing-gate, just in-field from a corner, join a wide grassy way to the left of further chalets. Farndon Bridge eventually comes into view; a string of kissing-gates leads you back to this and the adjacent car park. ●

the left edge of the next field and use a hand-gate to access a broad, hedge-lined track, Marsh Lane **B**. Turn left along this; at the nearby junction go ahead left for Churton, use the bridle-gate and remain on this sandy track past two remote cottages. Turn left along the subsequent tarred lane. At the junction turn right and walk to a sharp-right corner **C**.

Take the waymarked stile beside a field-gate on your immediate left (left of the hedged track) and walk across the narrow field to use a stiled footbridge. Walk along the left edge of the next

Gawsworth Hall and North Rode

		GPS waypoints
Start	Gawsworth, 4 miles south of Macclesfield	☑ SJ 886 694
Distance	6½ miles (10.5km)	**Ⓐ** SJ 891 697
Height gain	295 feet (90m)	**Ⓑ** SJ 906 697
Approximate time	3 hours	**Ⓒ** SJ 909 683
Parking	Gawsworth, Church Lane near the Harrington Arms	**Ⓓ** SJ 905 669
		Ⓔ SJ 900 668
Route terrain	Field paths, lanes, towpath; expect mud after decent rain	**Ⓕ** SJ 889 666
		Ⓖ SJ 889 677
Dog friendly	A few awkward stiles towards the end of the route	
Ordnance Survey maps	Landranger 118 (Stoke-on-Trent & Macclesfield), Explorer 268 (Wilmslow, Macclesfield & Congleton)	

This walk reveals the Cheshire landscape at its most typical. The surroundings of Gawsworth Hall and church at the start are particularly attractive and the route is undemanding and easy to follow, but be prepared for muddy conditions in places after wet weather.

✏ Start by the **Harrington Arms**, walk along the lane signposted to Gawsworth Church and the lane bends first left and then right. The views to the right across the pool to the church and black-and-white, half-timbered hall are outstanding. The mainly Elizabethan hall was the home of the Fitton family, one of whom, Mary Fitton, is thought to be the Dark Lady of Shakespeare's sonnets. There are Fitton family tombs in the 15th-century church whose imposing perpendicular tower rises to a height of 103 ft (31m).

At the far end of the pool **Ⓐ** turn right towards the gates to Gawsworth Hall. Swing left in front of these, tracing the lane past a rank of estate buildings to a sharp right bend. Leave the tarred lane here and continue ahead

on the rougher lane. At the brick entrance pillars to Pigeon House take the kissing-gate into the narrow neck of a pasture and walk alongside the hedge, right, as the field opens out. Two further kissing-gates lead to a low crest, from which excellent views stretch ahead to the conifers of Macclesfield Forest and the lonely ridge-top building that is the Cat & Fiddle Inn, second highest pub in England at 1,690ft (515m), whilst the wedge-shaped summit of Shutlingsloe rises behind Wincle Minn ridge. Remain beside the hedge, using more kissing-gates to reach a lane, along which bear right.

Turn right along Cowbrook Lane **Ⓑ**, signed for Bosley, walking above the railway cutting to your left. Remain on this lane over the railway and onwards for more than ½ mile to a bridge across the Macclesfield Canal **C**. Use the steps on the left just before this and turn right beneath the bridge, remaining on the towpath to reach the top lock of the Bosley flight **D**.

Use the walkers' gate beside the bridge here to gain a lane and turn right along this. Immediately across a railway bridge, the lane bends sharp right **E**;

here keep ahead on the driveway past an old lodge-house, signed as a bridlepath on a fingerpost beside stone gateposts.

Walk along a tarmac track – tree-lined in places – through the parkland adjoining North Rode Manor, pass by the end of the lake and just before a

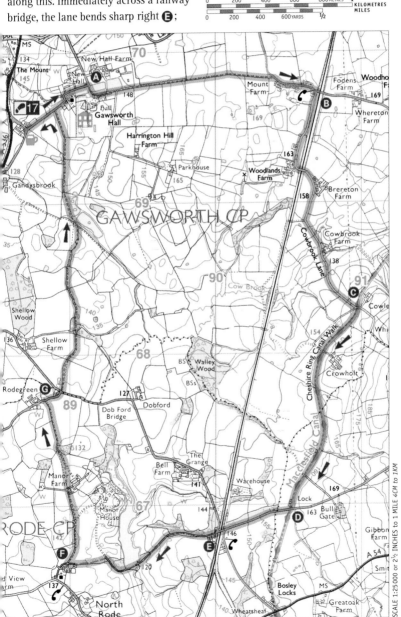

SCALE 1:25 000 or 2½ INCHES to 1 MILE 4CM to 1KM

Gawsworth church

gate and cattle-grid, bear left to a stile. Climb it, keep ahead towards a farm, joining the left field edge, climb a stile and walk along a track to a public footpath sign **F**. *Keep ahead along a tarmac track to see North Rode's Victorian church*; otherwise turn sharp right over a cattle-grid and along a concrete drive (signed 'Private Road'). At a fork, keep along the left-hand drive, go over a cattle-grid, pass to the left of a farm and climb the stile ahead.

Walk across a field, making for the left corner of the trees in front, where you pick up a track which curves right to a stile. Climb it, continue by the left edge of a field and climb another stile onto a lane. Turn right and at a T-junction, keep ahead over a stile **G** and walk along the left edge of a field. Climb a stile, continue along a left field edge, climb two stiles in quick succession and keep ahead to climb another one. Walk along the left edge of the next two fields – there are fine views ahead of Gawsworth church tower – and in the third field, bear slightly right across it to a stile in the corner. Climb it, continue in the same direction across the next field, climb a stile in front of lakes, immediately climb another one and turn left beside a lake.

At the causeway between lower and upper lakes, fork left on a path immediately beside the upper lake (on your right). At the far end take the grassy path slightly left up to a stile hidden beneath a huge holly tree. Once over this, continue along the left edge of a succession of fields to reach and descend a flight of steps down to Church Lane. Turn left to return to the nearby Harrington Arms. Make time to visit this unspoilt pub – the bar and tiny rooms are part of a working farmhouse. ●

Trent and Mersey Canal and Great Budworth

		GPS waypoints
Start	Marbury Country Park, just north of Northwich	
		🏁 SJ 652 763
Distance	7 miles (11.3km)	Ⓐ SJ 647 765
		Ⓑ SJ 640 756
Height gain	260 feet (80m)	Ⓒ SJ 643 752
Approximate time	3 hours	Ⓓ SJ 670 755
		Ⓔ SJ 672 758
Parking	Country Park (Pay & Display)	Ⓕ SJ 668 765
Route terrain	Field paths, roads and towpath; muddy in places after rain	Ⓖ SJ 664 769
		Ⓗ SJ 664 775
Ordnance Survey maps	Landranger 118 (Stoke-on-Trent & Macclesfield), Explorer 267 (Northwich & Delamere Forest)	Ⓙ SJ 654 774

There is plenty of historic interest on this walk as it starts at a former country estate and passes a unique monument to the Industrial Revolution and a medieval church. The route falls into three distinct segments. First comes a walk across fields to the canal at Anderton. This is followed by a 2½-mile stretch beside the Trent and Mersey Canal, passing the Anderton Boat Lift. More field walking leads first to the attractive village of Great Budworth and then back to the start. On the final stretch there are fine views over Budworth Mere.

Marbury Country Park, created in 1975, occupies the grounds of the former estate of the Marbury family, which was involved in the early salt industry of Northwich. After being requisitioned in the Second World War, the house was demolished in 1969.

🥾 Exit the car park beneath the carved wooden arch, walk past an information point to find a wide tarred track and turn left along this. Bend right past the Ranger's cabin and then left at the fingerpost to 'Bird Hide'. Remain on this old driveway, bend left and walk past the barrier to reach the main road, along which turn right.

Just past the bus shelter in 60 yds Ⓐ, take the waymarked stile, left, and walk along the right edge of a field to another stile. Climb it, keep ahead through trees, cross a footbridge over a stream and climb a stile to exit from the trees.

Walk across the next two fields, climbing two stiles, to emerge onto a lane. Climb the stile opposite, walk across a field, go through a wide gap and bear left along the left edge of the next field above a ditch. Climb a stile and continue along the right edge of fields, passing two redundant stiles before reaching a road Ⓑ. Turn left into Anderton and at a T-junction, turn sharp right over a canal bridge. Turn right through a hedge gap onto the

```
0    200   400   600   800 METRES  1
                                    KILOMETRES
                                    MILES
0    200   400   600 YARDS   ½
```

towpath and turn right again **C** to pass under the bridge.

Walk along the towpath of the Trent and Mersey Canal to the Anderton Boat Lift, an outstanding example of Victorian engineering. It was built in 1875 in order to transfer boats up or down the 50 ft from the River Weaver to the canal and was the first of its kind in the world. There is a visitor centre and a nature park reclaimed from industrial wasteland. On the other side of the river is a huge ICI complex. A bridge over the canal leads to the pub on the opposite bank.

Continue by the canal – soon the woodlands of Marbury Country Park are

seen over to the left – as far as bridge No.193 and turn right in front of it up to a road **D**. **The Salt Barge** pub and Lion Salt Works Museum are to the right. The route continues to the left over the bridge and between flashes, the latter caused by subsidence. Immediately past the compound, turn left on a rough lane **E**. At the far end pass to the right of the fence to reach a stile. Climb this and trace the right edge of the next field to use a further stile. From here, head half-right (towards the distant houses) to two gates and a stile in a wide gap in the far hedgerow **F**. Climb the stile at the sharp point of a field and put a fence on your left, heading just left of the houses. Cross a track via two stiles and then keep the

along the pavement. After 400 yds turn right at a fingerpost and walk up the sloping field to put the top hedge on your left. Excellent views stretch ahead to the Peak District. Walk on to use a stile into a grassy track. This shortly becomes a tarred lane; turn left to the centre of Great Budworth at the **George & Dragon** pub. Take time to visit the fine medieval church here **H**.

Turn left down High Street to a crossroads. Carefully cross straight over into Budworth Lane (for Comberbach and Runcorn). In about ½ mile, take the waymarked path **J** into the woods on your left, just past Brownslow Cottage. At the far side of the woods, use the kissing-gate and keep ahead to pick up the line of a fence on your right. Budworth Mere is off to your left; go through another kissing-gate, cross a footbridge and keep ahead with another fence on your right to use a further kissing-gate.

Again keep ahead to find a final kissing-gate onto a pavement. Turn left, then left again along the driveway to Marbury Hall Nurseries. Keep ahead at the barrier, from here retracing your route back to the car park. ●

hedgerow on your right, crossing another stile before reaching a main road **G**.

Carefully cross the road and turn left

Great Budworth

Beeston Castle and the Shropshire Union Canal

		GPS waypoints
Start	Beeston Castle	〉 SJ 540 590
Distance	6½ miles (10.5km)	Ⓐ SJ 538 602
Height gain	425 feet (130m)	Ⓑ SJ 509 602
Approximate time	3 hours	Ⓒ SJ 518 577
Parking	Beeston Castle car park (free for castle visitors, note closing time)	Ⓓ SJ 525 575
		Ⓔ SJ 528 575
Route terrain	Towpath, field paths and lanes; one gentle climb, muddy in Pennsylvania Wood	Ⓕ SJ 535 583
Ordnance Survey maps	Landranger 117 (Chester & Wrexham), Explorers 257 (Crewe & Nantwich) and 267 (Northwich & Delamere Forest)	

For most of the walk, there are striking views both of medieval Beeston Castle and Victorian Peckforton Castle, perched on neighbouring wooded hills overlooking the Cheshire plain. Much of the route is flat but towards the end, a gentle climb through Pennsylvania Wood brings you onto the sandstone ridge followed by a walk through woodland along the ridge. After descending, the final stretch across fields brings views of Beeston Castle.

Beeston Castle has one of the most dramatic locations of any castle in the country, occupying the summit of a wooded hill which rises abruptly above the Cheshire plain. The mainly 13th-century fortress, one of the strongholds of the powerful earls of Chester, was built to protect the English border. In spite of its apparently impregnable position, it was successfully captured by a small Royalist force from its Parliamentary occupants in the Civil War.

Crowning the adjoining summit is Peckforton Castle, built in the middle of the 19th century as an almost perfect replica of a 12th-century fortress, a superb example of the desire of many wealthy Victorians to recreate medieval buildings and ideals.

From the car park turn right along the lane. Pass by a junction and Castlegate Farm and then look for a kissing-gate and Sandstone Trail fingerpost on the right. Go left along the wide field road, look for a waymarked stile on the right beside two trees and a gate, climb this and turn left beside the fence. At the field foot climb a stile and head half-left to an underpass beneath the railway. Use kissing-gates either end of this and then follow the walked path slightly left, cross a flat bridge over a drain and walk to the first kissing-gate Ⓐ.

Join the canal here at Wharton's Lock and turn left, passing beneath Bridge No. 108. Remain on the towpath of the Shropshire Union Canal for the next 2 miles, shortly passing the **Shady Oak** pub on the far bank. Look for where the canal bends sharply left – on the right is an overspill weir, on your left some pine trees . At this juncture look carefully for a narrow, steep, railed path down to your left (if you reach the canal's right bend, you've gone too far). Descend this via a hand-gate to reach a path, along which turn right on a tree-lined path – here joining the Eddisbury Way – to a stile. Climb it, keep ahead along the right edge of a field and just after passing a gate in the hedge on the right, bear left diagonally across the field and turn left over a stile in the far corner.

Walk along an enclosed track which bends right to a T-junction, turn right and at a public footpath sign immediately after passing under a railway bridge, turn left up steps and climb a stile. Bear slightly right across a field, making for the left side of a tree-

Beeston Castle

fringed pool, climb a stile and continue in the same direction across the next field to a stile.

Climb it, turn left along a fence-lined track and where it bends right, go ahead over a stile. Bear diagonally right across a field, climb a stile through a wire fence and almost immediately cross a stiled footbridge on your left. Turn right along the right edge of a field, cross a footbridge in the corner, keep along the right edge of the next field and look out for where you turn right over a stile onto a lane. Turn left to a T-junction, turn left and almost immediately turn right along Wood Lane. Where the lane bends left, continue along first a tarmac track and then a cobbled track and where the track bends left to a farm, keep ahead over a stone stile **C**.

Walk across a field towards a waymarked stile but before reaching it, turn left over a stile to the left of a gate and turn right along the right edge of a field. Cross a footbridge over a brook and bear right to climb a stile on the edge of Pennsylvania Wood. Follow a path uphill along the left inside edge of the trees and after going through a gate, continue through the wood. In about 300 yds the gently rising path swings left beneath fir trees and across a plank bridge, shortly reaching a track **D**. Cross the track and join a path just inside the woods, signposted for Peckforton and Beeston Moss. Pass through a gap in a woodland fence and then climb a stile, shortly

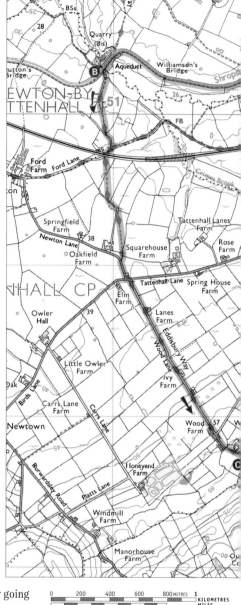

reaching the edge of the trees. Turn left along the track bending left from the cottage, shortly reaching a crossways within the woodland fringe **E**.

Turn left on the Sandstone Trail for Beeston Castle. The track continues through delightful woodland below

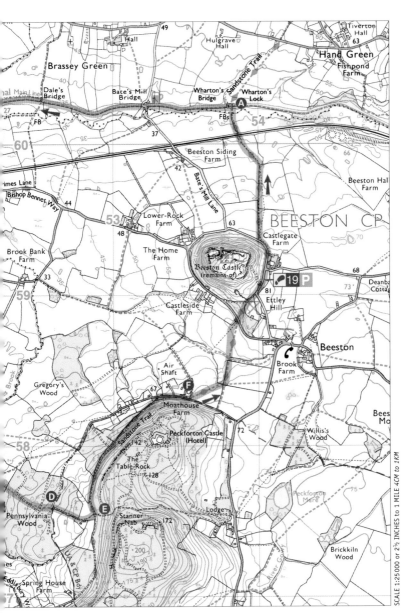

Peckforton Castle (not visible). Views on the left stretch to Chester's cathedral. The track eventually meets a tarred lane. Turn right and at a Sandstone Trail fingerpost for Beeston Castle use the kissing-gate on your left **F**, then walk the wide field path to another kissing-gate in the far corner. Turn left to a track along the edge of the field and walk to and across a footbridge in a belt of trees. Use the kissing-gate and continue on the obvious field path to another kissing-gate and steps down to a lane.

Look left for a gap stile into the woods opposite, use it and climb the path through fir woods. Keep left along the top edge, walk along the enclosed path and bear left along the lane to return to the start.

●

Caldy Hill, Thurstaston and the Wirral Way

		GPS waypoints
Start	Wirral Way, Thurstaston Visitor Centre, signposted from A540 at Thurstaston	🏁 SJ 239 834
		Ⓐ SJ 222 849
		Ⓑ SJ 224 853
Distance	7¼ miles (11.6km)	Ⓒ SJ 223 855
Height gain	445 feet (135m)	Ⓓ SJ 232 860
Approximate time	3½ hours	Ⓔ SJ 242 861
Parking	Visitor Centre (free)	Ⓕ SJ 247 841
Route terrain	Old railway lanes and field paths; may be muddy in places. Two short, easy climbs	Ⓖ SJ 252 832
		Ⓗ SJ 245 828
Ordnance Survey maps	Landranger 108 (Liverpool), Explorer 266 (Wirral & Chester)	

The opening and closing stretches are along the Wirral Way beside the Dee Estuary. Much of the remainder of the route is through broadleaf woodland and across sandy heathland. There is a series of superb viewpoints but the finest is the summit of Thurstaston Hill which, despite its modest height, 299 ft (91m), offers views over the Dee and Mersey estuaries.

Wirral Country Park Visitor Centre at Thurstaston is situated on a grassy clifftop above the Dee Estuary and there are fine views across the water to the hills of North Wales. The Wirral Way, a footpath and cycleway, uses the track of a former railway which ran along the western side of the Wirral.

🏁 From the car park find the old platform and turn right, almost immediately passing beneath Station Road bridge. Remain with this old railway trackbed for 1¼ miles to the point where it descends a ramp to reach a lane Ⓐ. The way is right here. Going left for 110 yds brings you to a viewpoint across the Dee Estuary. From the ramp, turn right and fork left at the junction along Croft Drive West,

bending right with this to a junction. Turn sharp left and after 100 yds look carefully on your right for a fingerpost showing the entrance to a narrow, fenced path that rises to another road Ⓑ. Turn left and walk to the hairpin bend. The route is right, but take time to divert along the finger-posted path on the left. Pass through an open stone gateway, take the first right and then keep ahead up a steep path to reach a small clearing and a bench, from which modest height on Caldy Hill Ⓒ are fine views to the Hilbre Islands and across to the North Wales coast.

Return to the hairpin bend and turn uphill, winding round to a junction with Thorsway. Keep right here along Kings Drive and walk to its end at a barrier into woodland. Take the path directly ahead (not left), a meandering route through the beautiful Stapledon Wood that eventually emerges into a cul-de-sac before reaching a road. Turn right and walk to the foot of the hill, looking for Grange Cross Road on the left; turn into this.

In 100 yds look for the narrow finger-posted stile on the right **D**, leading into an enclosed path through to a stile.

Keep ahead on the tree-lined path (ponds to your right), at the end of which drift left to a field-side path rising to a stone stile into a track. Follow the track around first a right bend and then a left bend to reach a road and turn right. At a public footpath sign to Thurstaston, turn left along a tree-lined track **E** to enter Royden Park. This former Victorian

Thurstaston Hall

estate, together with the adjoining Thurstaston Common, comprise a large public access area of woodland, heathland and parkland. On reaching a tarmac track, Royden Park Visitor Centre is ahead but you turn right on the tarred lane. Take the path just past the tarred track on the left, a woodland path signed for Thurstaston Common. After 50 yds at a fork keep ahead on the lesser path under a low bower of holly, putting an overflow car park to your left. Remain on the narrow path within the trees, parallel to an open grassy area, to reach a short stretch of stone wall. Turn right for a few paces and then turn left to find a National Trust sign and board.

Take the path immediately right of this, tracing this gently rising way across heathland and through scrubby birch woods, eventually using a kissing-gate before continuing ahead to pass by Benty Farm on your left. In a further 100 yds the track bends left beneath overhead wires. At this point, fork ahead – bear right along the narrow path directly beneath the wires, walking through to a kissing-gate into the top of a lane.

Bear right and go up three steps to climb the short distance to the triangulation pillar and viewfinder on the summit of Thurstaston Hill. The views from here are tremendous, taking in the buildings of Liverpool, the Wirral and the hills of North Wales. In clear conditions they extend to the Great Orme and the Snowdonia range.

Retrace your steps to the bottom of the hill, turn sharp right along a track and go through a kissing-gate onto a road. Bear left into Thurstaston; at a crossroads just past the **Cottage Loaf** pub turn right on Station Road, then left at the T-junction **F** along a lane, passing left of the red sandstone Victorian church. In the churchyard is the early 19th-century tower of its predecessor. Where the lane bends left, keep ahead along a track at a public footpath sign to Heswall to a stile. Climb it, continue along an enclosed path, negotiating a kissing-gate and several stiles, and after reaching a footpath post in a belt of trees, turn right, in the Wirral Way direction **G**. The path heads gently downhill through the lovely wooded dell of The Dungeon to a waymarked post.

Turn left to descend steps, turn right, head up an embankment and turn right to rejoin the Wirral Way **H**. In front of gates, bear left along a path which bends left to a T-junction, turn right and follow a track back to the start. ●

Wirral Way, Parkgate and the Dee Estuary

		GPS waypoints	
Start	Hadlow Road old station, Willaston	📝	SJ 330 773
Distance	8¼ miles (13.2km)	**A**	SJ 297 773
		B	SJ 280 778
Height gain	245 feet (75m)	**C**	SJ 285 766
Approximate time	3½ hours	**D**	SJ 291 758
		E	SJ 301 760
Parking	Hadlow Road station (free)	**F**	SJ 304 768
Route terrain	Old railway, lanes and field paths	**G**	SJ 310 772
Ordnance Survey maps	Landranger 117 (Chester & Wrexham), Explorer 266 (Wirral & Chester)		

Much of the route is along the Wirral Way, a former railway track, which provides easy and pleasant walking along tree-lined embankments and through deep cuttings. In complete contrast, the middle stretch, between Parkgate and Little Neston, takes you along the edge of the extensive marshes bordering the Dee Estuary, from where there are superb views looking across to the hills of North Wales.

Wirral Country Park is based around the Wirral Way, a disused railway track. Most of the track was converted into a footpath and bridleway after the railway closed down in the 1960s. The railway, built in 1865, ran along the western side of the Wirral and the station at Hadlow Road has been preserved as it was in 1952, with the original waiting room, ticket office and signal box.

📝 Begin by walking along the platform of the former station, go through a gate, cross the road and take the track opposite to join the Wirral Way. Follow it for the next 2 miles – along the top of tree-lined embankments and later through a deep sandstone cutting – to reach a road in Neston **A**. Here the track has been obliterated and the route continues

along Station Road. Where the road ends, continue ahead beneath the railway bridge; then shortly fork left along the tarred path (National Cycle Route 56). This crosses an iron bridge over a road before reforming as the old railway line.

Follow it for another ¾ mile, eventually passing beside a gate and continuing along a tarmac track to a road in Parkgate. Turn left to a T-junction in front of the Dee estuary **B**. The village centre, which has a pleasantly old-fashioned and rather abandoned air about it, is to the right. In the 18th century, Parkgate was an important port with a flourishing passenger trade across the estuary to Wales and with Ireland. But the relentless silting up of the Dee, which had earlier destroyed Chester as a port,

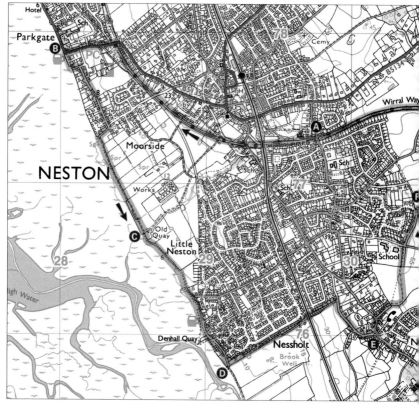

continued and Parkgate's prosperity declined. It enjoyed a brief revival in the 19th century as a holiday resort and The Parade, lined with 17th- to 19th-century buildings, still retains something of the atmosphere of a fashionable promenade.

At the T-junction the route continues to the left. Where the road peters out, keep ahead along a paved path above the marshes and the path bends left to emerge onto a tarmac drive. Turn right, pass beside a barrier to continue along a fence-lined path, pass beside another barrier and keep ahead along Manorial Road South. At a junction, turn right beside a barrier and walk along a grassy enclosed path that bends sharp left (not the one by the spout) to continue beside the marshes of the estuary again. There are fine views across the estuary to the hills of North Wales and the walls and

towers of Flint Castle can be seen. Initially this part of the walk is likely to be muddy at times but later a paved path leads to a stile.

Climb it, veer slightly left to continue along the top of a low embankment, cross a footbridge over a stream and keep ahead to climb a stone stile at Old Quay **C**. The broken walls here are among a number of remains of former wharves along this part of the estuary. Continue at first along a path by the edge of the marshes and as you join a track, the coal tip to the left is a reminder that there was once a colliery here. Pass in front of houses to reach the **Harp Inn**, continue past the pub and at a fence corner just beyond the last of the houses on the left, turn left along a tarmac path where the way ahead is restricted by bollards **D**.

Simply remain with this tarred path

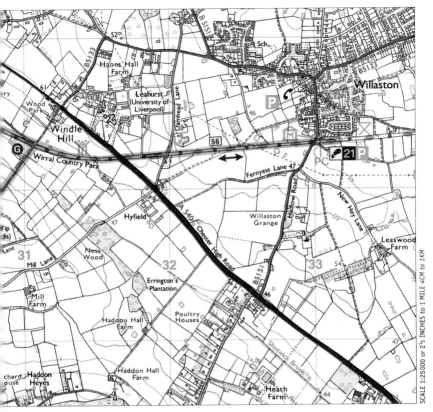

(cutting a corner on a dirt path), keeping housing to your left. Pass by a barrier, continuing to rise gradually and walk beneath a railway bridge, beyond which a wider, hedged track climbs to reach a lane. Turn right on this, walking through to a crossroads in the centre of Ness **E**. Turn left; pass **The Wheatsheaf** pub and then turn right along the narrow Cumbers Lane. Where the track bends left, keep ahead along an enclosed path. After going up two steps, the way continues across a field, following a path which curves left to a stile on the far side. Climb it, walk along the left edge of a playing field to a lane and keep ahead along Gorstons Lane. Just before a junction, turn right, **F** at a public bridleway sign, along a

hedged track. After 400 yds this bends left, gently falling to reach an over-bridge **G**. Immediately before this, use the stile, left, and climb up to the old railway line. Turn right to return to Hadlow Road old station. ●

Parkgate

Above Helsby and Frodsham

Above Helsby and Frodsham

		GPS waypoints
Start	Helsby Quarry Woodland Park on Helsby Hill	⬚ SJ 490 749
Distance	7 miles (11.3km)	Ⓐ SJ 499 748
		Ⓑ SJ 508 747
Height gain	870 feet (265m)	Ⓒ SJ 512 755
Approximate time	3½ hours	Ⓓ SJ 519 753
		Ⓔ SJ 520 769
Parking	Helsby Quarry Woodland Park (free)	Ⓕ SJ 514 762
		Ⓖ SJ 505 757
Route terrain	Hilly, with lots of climbs and descents. May be muddy in woodland	Ⓗ SJ 497 758
Ordnance Survey maps	Landranger 117 (Chester & Wrexham), Explorer 267 (Northwich & Delamere Forest)	

The sandstone ridge which runs north to south across Cheshire ends abruptly at steep wooded cliffs that plunge down to the adjacent towns of Helsby and Frodsham. These cliffs overlook the River Mersey and there are a series of dramatic views over the estuary. This is quite an energetic route, with a lot of ascents and descents – some of them steep – and some fairly difficult walking in places along rocky, winding and uneven paths across the thickly-wooded cliffsides.

Walk up Hill Road South (almost opposite the car park) to a stile at the top end, just past a gate. Go through this and into the National Trust's Helsby Hill property. The path curves right, continues uphill and at a fork, take the right-hand path, signed for Harmers Lake, passing between rock faces then past a pond on your left. Bear right down the tarred lane which heads downhill past woodland and bends left. At a public footpath sign to 'Tarvin Road and Sandstone Trail' turn right through a gate into a fenced path and walk to a kissing-gate. Turn left through this to reach and use another kissing-gate, whereupon trace the left,

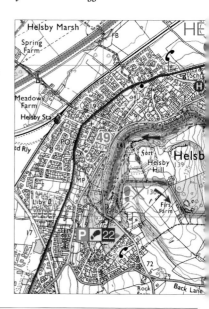

then bottom edges of the sloping pasture to use a further kissing-gate in the corner. Beyond here, walk the tree-shaded path to a road **A**.

Turn left and after 200 yds use the kissing-gate on the right, signed for Burrow. Walk the right edge of this field, cross to the other side of the hedge at a kissing-gate and footbridge and walk the left edge of a long field, joining a rough field-side track running via a gate to a kissing-gate into a lane. Turn left, at a T-junction turn right and at a public footpath sign to Woodhouse Hill and Frodsham, bear left along a tree-lined track **B**. Regular Sandstone Trail discs confirm the way up this secluded woodland valley, presently

reaching a bench and T-junction **C**. Turn right, leaving the Sandstone Trail in favour of a rising, occasionally stepped path to and beyond the wood's edge, continuing up a rough track to reach a road **D**. Turn left; after 200 yds use the waymarked kissing-gate, left, and head half-right for the wooded corner. Cross the farm lane and join the waymarked Delamere Way, an enclosed path beside a golf course, which eventually issues into a pasture; trace the left edge to reach a lane and turn left.

In 150 yds turn right along the rough

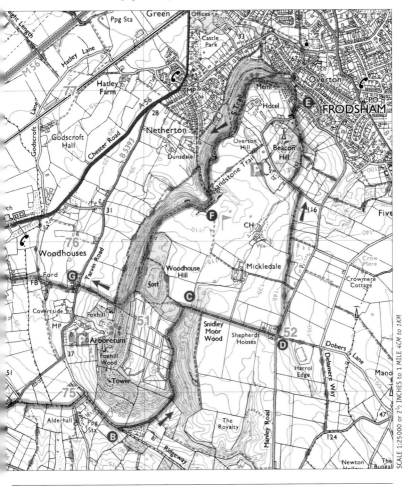

SCALE 1:25000 or 2½ INCHES to 1 MILE 4CM to 1KM

track for Overhill Cottage. As this bends left, keep ahead on the grassy path to a gate. Cross the tarred drive and follow the waymarked path through woodland, then bracken to gain a lane. Turn right to the **Belle Monte Hotel**, 100 yds downhill .

At the inside corner of the car park look for the narrow waymarked path into the woods. Within yards, keep left on the upper path, then shortly left again on the Sandstone Trail for Delamere and Beeston. In a short distance turn left up steps to emerge on Frodsham Hill top next to the war memorial, from which point are exceptional views across the Mersey to Liverpool, the Wirral and many distant marks featured on the nearby toposcope. Walk past this plaque and along a path through gorse and bracken; at a fork take the waymarked Sandstone Trail down to the right, tracing the well-waymarked trail through the top of the woods.

On reaching a fingerpost , turn right for Delamere Forest. Drop down steps and follow the path left to reach a long flight of steps. Turn right at the foot of these, then left at the junction in a glade, again signed for Delamere Forest. Cross a footbridge across the top of a gulch, shortly after which scramble up a rock-face, continuing then within the woods beside a golf course, eventually reaching a bench and viewpoint over Helsby Hill.

Just beyond the bench, keep right at a waymarked junction of paths, leaving the Sandstone Trail here. The path soon reaches a junction at the corner of a

The Mersey Estuary from Mickledale

fenced meadow; turn right. Ignore the gate into Woodhouse Hill Wood, instead start to descend on a steep, braided path across tree roots, eventually reaching a kissing-gate onto a lane. Walk down this to the main road .

Turn left and then go right down Chestnut Lane. Beyond the cottages, cross a footbridge and use the kissing-gate to enter rough pasture; walk ahead to find a narrow, enclosed path. At the far end of this, cross the top of a lane, use another kissing-gate (signed Bates Lane) and head half-right up the field to another gate and a narrow, fenced path. At the end turn right down a lane to reach a crossroads .

Turn left along Old Chester Road. Very shortly, take the fingerposted path, left, for Helsby Hill. At the top, take the stile signed for Middle Walk and Hill Top, entering the National Trust's Helsby Hill property again. Immediately fork right and then shortly left onto an undulating path through woods across the flank of Helsby Hill. Pass by a gate to reach a lane; turn left up this to find the car park just around a left-bend. ●

Mow Cop and Little Moreton Hall

		GPS waypoints
Start	Mow Cop	
Distance	7½ miles (12km) Shorter walk 5 miles (8km)	✎ SJ 856 573
		Ⓐ SJ 859 576
		Ⓑ SJ 846 589
Height gain	820 feet (250m). Shorter version 720 feet (220m)	Ⓒ SJ 843 584
		Ⓓ SJ 832 588
Approximate time	3½ hours (2½ hours for shorter walk)	Ⓔ SJ 848 594
		Ⓕ SJ 860 592
Parking	National Trust car park at Mow Cop folly (free) narrow entrance	Ⓖ SJ 861 596
		Ⓗ SJ 867 592
Route terrain	Lanes, towpath and field paths; muddy in places. May be very marshy at Ⓗ. One long steady climb	Ⓙ SJ 864 582
Dog friendly	Lots of stiles on the route	
Ordnance Survey maps	Landranger 118 (Stoke-on-Trent & Macclesfield), Explorer 268 (Wilmslow, Macclesfield & Congleton)	

Starting on a ridge, the route descends across fields and through woodland to the Macclesfield Canal. It then continues to Little Moreton Hall before returning to the canal. Then comes a steady climb to regain the ridge, offering fine views through 360°. The shorter version omits the extension to Little Moreton Hall.

The 'castle' at Mow Cop is a folly, a mock ruin built by a local landowner in 1754 to enhance the view. At a meeting on this summit in 1807 the Primitive Methodist movement was born.

✎ At a Gritstone Trail sign, take the path towards the left of the folly, at a fork continue along the left-hand path to a track and bear left to a road. Turn right and at a Gritstone Trail fingerpost turn left along a track which bends left, in front of houses and then turns right to pass to the left of the Old Man, a rock pinnacle created by quarrying. At a fingerpost just in front of a radio mast, Ⓐ turn left – following South Cheshire Way signs – and head gently downhill,

by a wire fence on the left, to a stile. Climb it, keep along the left edge of two fields, before climbing a stile into woodland, and continue downhill to a T-junction. Turn left to climb a stile at the edge of the trees, turn right downhill along the right edge of a field and at a hedge corner, keep ahead across the field to a gate.

Go through the hand-gate, walk downhill and bear left down the rough lane. At a T-junction fork right, signed for Ackers Crossing, and continue down the lane. At the next junction, turn left along the tarred lane, shortly using the kissing-gate on the left to access an underpass beneath the railway. At the far side bear left to a junction at a green. Bear right, soon crossing a bridge over the Macclesfield Canal. Cross the bridge and immediately drop down the steps on your right to join the towpath.

For the shorter walk, turn left along the towpath **B**.

For the extension to Little Moreton Hall, turn right beneath Bridge No. 85 and walk the towpath to Bridge No. 86. Go under this and immediately use the two kissing-gates on your right to join a field road **C**.

Turn left along it and follow it to the point where it gives out at a field corner between two trees. Climb the narrow stile here and join a fenced path along the right edge of a huge field. Climb two more field-edge stiles. Once over the second of these, head half-left across pasture towards the farm buildings. Further stiles land you on a tarred drive; keep ahead to reach Little Moreton Hall **D**.

This is one of the most photographed houses in England, its picturesque quality admired by producers of birthday cards and calendars. It was built in the late 15th to 16th centuries

Mow Cop folly

as the home of the Moreton family, local gentry, and has remained virtually unaltered since Elizabethan times.

Retrace your steps to Bridge No. 85 **C**, rejoin the shorter walk and continue north along the towpath. After passing under Bridge No. 83, turn left up steps to a lane **E**, cross the canal bridge and follow the lane across a railway bridge, around a sharp left-bend and on to a junction where Oak Lane joins from the left. Here turn right up a tarred lane. On reaching barns on either side of the lane **F**, turn left along a muddy track just within the woodland (note half-hidden fingerpost here). Remain on this track close to the woodland edge to reach a boggy corner where duck-boarding leads to a stile. Climb it, turn right along the field edge and look carefully after about 150 yds for a low, waymarked post pointing the way, right, down overgrown steps **G**.

Cross three plank bridges and a stile and then stay on the path in the woods, rising gradually above the brook to use a stile beside a gate. Walk ahead on the track past Corda Well Cottage. Just past

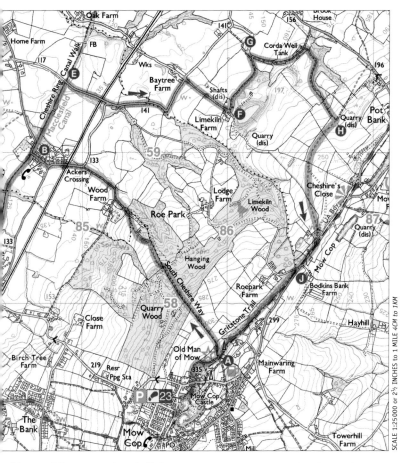

SCALE 1:25000 or 2½ INCHES to 1 MILE 4CM to 1KM

this turn right up a track and climb a gate-side stile into a sloping field. Trace the sinuous edge of the woods all the way up, climb another gate-side stile and walk uphill beside an unkempt hedge on your right.

This turns right at a corner marked by a low waymarked post **H**. Turn right here along a distinct embankment, leading to a stile through a tall hedge. Keep in the same direction to climb another stile. Beyond this, walk along a track curving left. This disappears into a reedy and potentially marshy area of upland pasture. Choose a route to take you past the top end of the strand of alder trees at the far-right side of this boggy area, climb a stile onto a drive and walk up this to a ridge-top road.

Turn right, enjoying the views left towards the Peak District and right, across Cheshire to the hills of North Wales and the West Pennines.

On your right is the driveway to Roe Park Farm **J**. At the corner here, a Gritstone Trail fingerpost points the way through a kissing-gate and onto a path that winds within the top edge of scrubby birch woods. Beyond the woods, pass alongside a low quarried bank on your left, use a gap-stile and climb the path that passes just right of the telephone mast. At a T-junction turn right along the Gritstone Trail to return to the start. ●

Timbersbrook and The Cloud

		GPS waypoints
Start	Timbersbrook, about 2 miles east of Congleton	◪ SJ 894 627
Distance	6½ miles (10.4km). Two shorter options of 4¼ miles (6.8km) and 2½ miles (4km)	Ⓐ SJ 886 623 Ⓑ SJ 880 626 Ⓒ SJ 880 630 Ⓓ SJ 891 630
Height gain	950 feet (290m). Two shorter options 705 feet (215m) and 245 feet (75m)	Ⓔ SJ 898 629 Ⓕ SJ 904 636 Ⓖ SJ 910 621
Approximate time	3½ hours (2 hours and 1½ hours for shorter options)	Ⓗ SJ 903 621 Ⓙ SJ 896 628
Parking	Timbersbrook picnic area (free)	
Route terrain	Lanes, field paths and towpath; muddy in places. One long steady climb	
Ordnance Survey maps	Landranger 118 (Stoke-on-Trent & Macclesfield), Explorer 268 (Wilmslow, Macclesfield & Congleton)	

A walk to the Macclesfield Canal is followed by a climb of The Cloud, 1,125 ft (343m) high and a magnificent viewpoint. There are fine and contrasting views, both across the Cheshire plain and the hills and moors of the Peak District. Almost a figure-of-eight, the route can be divided into two shorter walks: the 4¼ mile walk, an ascent of The Cloud; the 2½ mile one omits The Cloud but includes the canal.

Timbersbrook is so green and quiet nowadays that it is almost impossible to envisage it as a noisy industrial area, the site of the Silver Springs Bleaching and Dyeing Company works. There is an information board in the car park.

◪ Begin by turning right out of the car park along a lane. Just after crossing a brook, turn left along a track, at a public footpath sign, joining both the Gritstone Trail and also the Staffordshire Way.

If doing the 4¼mile walk, instead continue along the lane and rejoin the full walk at point Ⓓ.

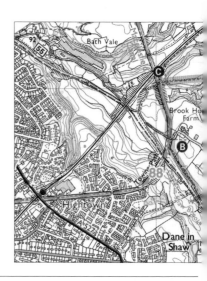

After passing in front of a house, keep ahead along a path to the left of a converted mill, drop to cross a footbridge over Timbers Brook then use a kissing-gate. Walk slightly left across the field to another kissing-gate; beyond this keep ahead to use a further kissing-gate just past a deep gulch. Turn right and then left along the line of oaks to find a fourth kissing-gate. Beyond this, walk ahead beside a fence, left, to a hand-gate, cross the drive and use three stiles in quick succession, thereby reaching a lane **Ⓐ**.

Turn right; in 100 yds turn left at a Gritstone Trail fingerpost through a concreted farmyard. Go through a gate and continue along an enclosed track. Climb a stone stile, walk along the right edge of a field and in the corner, turn right over a stile. Keep along the left edge of the next field, parallel to a disused railway track on the left, continue along the left edge of the next

two fields, finally climbing a stile and descending steps to the Macclesfield Canal **Ⓑ**.

Turn right beside it and after going through a gate, turn left to cross a canal bridge. Immediately turn left through a gate, go down steps and turn sharp left to pass under the bridge. Continue beside the canal and just before the next bridge (No. 71), turn left up to a T-junction **Ⓒ**. Turn right to cross the bridge and keep ahead along a path through trees to enter a field. Ahead are superb views of The Cloud. Continue across the undulating field, bearing slightly right to pass through a neck of woodland before making for the far-right corner. Climb a stile and walk the track through to a hand-gate into a lane.

Turn right to return to the start if

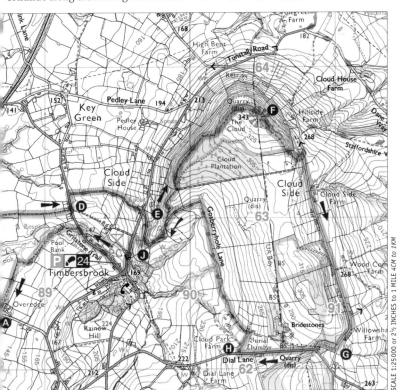

The Bridestones

doing the 2 ½ mile walk.

For the full walk **D**, turn left and at a public footpath sign, turn right beside a gate, here rejoining the Staffordshire Way, and head gently uphill along a tree-lined track (Acorn Lane). The track later heads more steeply uphill to a road. Cross over, continue along the uphill track ahead (Gosberryhole Lane) through trees and follow it round a left bend to a fork just past a secluded house **E**.

Fork left through a gap stile and past a National Trust sign, 'The Cloud'. At a split keep left and continue uphill, curving right, pass beside a fence, at a Gritstone Trail waymark, and follow the direction of the waymark – there are several paths here – uphill along a track to emerge from the trees onto heathery moorland.

Follow the winding path uphill through the heather to the triangulation pillar on the summit **F**. This magnificent and contrasting all-round viewpoint includes the hills and moors of the eastern Peak District, the Cheshire plain, Congleton, Macclesfield and Jodrell Bank. Beyond the summit, the path bears right to continue along the edge, descending gently. After passing through a fence gap, walk along an enclosed path, descend steps to a T-junction and turn left along a track which bends right to a lane.

Turn right and after ¾ mile, take the first lane on the right **G** which curves left to reach an often busy road. Turn right and after 250 yds turn right again along the second driveway to view the Bridestones prehistoric burial chamber (on your left in bushes). Return to the main road and turn downhill. After 200 yds turn right **H** along a narrow lane. Bend left at the farm entrance and then walk ahead on the sandy track as the tarred lane turns left; this is Gosberryhole Lane. Simply remain with this peaceful byway to and past **E**. Just after the track bends right, take the waymarked Gritstone Trail to the left, down a long, steep flight of wooden steps and through to a lane **J**. Turn left down this and after 200 yds take the waymarked gap stile on the right, descend steps and walk the path into the car park. ●

Shutlingsloe

Start	Trentabank car park, on minor road east of Langley (signs for Macclesfield Forest & Wildboarclough)	GPS waypoints
		✎ SJ 961 711
		Ⓐ SJ 971 703
		Ⓑ SJ 976 695
Distance	6½ miles (10.5km)	Ⓒ SJ 982 685
Height gain	1,280 feet (390m)	Ⓓ SJ 962 687
Approximate time	3½ hours	Ⓔ SJ 961 694
		Ⓕ SJ 952 696
Parking	Car park next to Visitor Centre (Pay and Display)	Ⓖ SJ 955 710
Route terrain	Forestry tracks, moorland paths, lanes and fields. One long, steady climb	
Ordnance Survey maps	Landranger 118 (Stoke-on-Trent & Macclesfield), Explorer OL1 (The Peak District – Dark Peak area)	

Shutlingsloe's distinctive appearance earns it the title 'Cheshire Matterhorn'. The climb – initially through the conifers of Macclesfield Forest and later over open moorland – is steady rather than steep and strenuous and is mostly on paved paths. After descending into Wildboarclough, the remainder of the route contours around the sides of the hill, before the final descent into the forest. Choose a fine and clear day as the views from these westerly fringes of the Peak District are immense.

✎ Take the path left of the Ranger's Office and parallel to the lane. Keep ahead through the green anti-bike gate to reach a kissing-gate on your left. The main route heads right here; a short diversion across the lane on your left leads to a viewing area across to Cheshire's largest heronry (best in late spring). Return to the main route and join the path for Shutlingsloe. This rises beside a wall on your right; go ahead over a major cross-track and continue by the wall through Macclesfield Forest. At a fork beyond a gate keep ahead-left; in another 400 yds fork right off this forestry road onto the Shutlingsloe path, shortly reaching a kissing-gate onto the open moor Ⓐ.

Join the paved path and rise with it across the flank of the moor. Once over a rise, the distinctive summit of Shutlingsloe is revealed ahead; simply remain with the well-used path, presently tackling the short, steep climb to the sharp peak.

Views from the summit can, on clear days, be immense – west across Cheshire to the mountains of north-east Wales, north to the West Pennine moors, east to the Cat & Fiddle and Shining Tor (Cheshire's highest point) and south along the ridge to distant Mow Cop.

Leave the summit triangulation pillar Ⓑ via a very steep path that drops eastwards towards the deep, wooded valley of Clough Brook. The well-walked path drops to a stile and hand-gate; use this and continue downhill past waymark posts. Climb another stile, cross some boardwalk and trace the line of wall on your right through a gap and onto a tarred farm driveway. Bear right and walk the narrow lane down to a road in the valley bottom; turn right along this to reach the **Crag Inn** at Wildboarclough **C**.

At the far car park entrance take the waymarked hand-gate beside a field-gate and bear left along the obvious ledged path, rising gradually through and past gorse to find a hand-gate through a wall. This is the first of a series of such gates; simply contour-walk across the fields using the gates as you find them. At a hand-gate well below the farm on your right, pass through and head half-right to reach a crossing of a brook, beyond which trace a cattle trod around the hillside. Use a stile, pass beneath a line of cables and look ahead right to sight a fingerpost on top of a walled embankment. Passing between tall old gateposts, walk to this.

Turn left along the tarred lane,

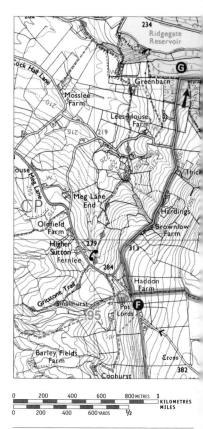

In Macclesfield Forest

dropping gradually to a junction. Here bear right to drop to Greenway Bridge, across Highmoor Brook **D**. Take the waymarked stile on the right, joining a path that follows the course of the brook upstream along a secluded little valley. Climb a stile, cross a flat bridge and then head slightly left, passing a section of broken walling. At a waymark post fork left, rejoining a good path up a reedy valley, a watercourse again on your left. The well-formed track reaches a green and white waymark disc

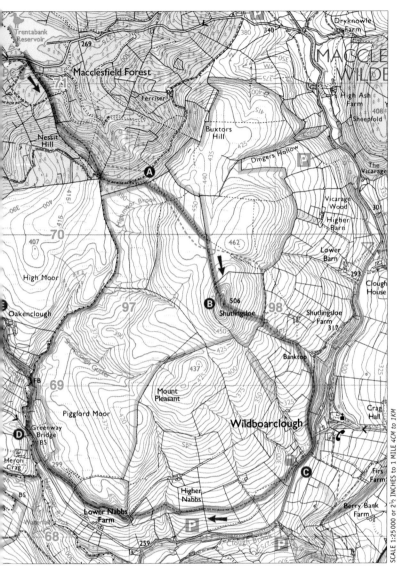

SCALE 1:25000 or 2½ INCHES to 1 MILE 4CM to 1KM

below a remote house. Bear left, pass between concrete gateposts, cross the streamlet and then bear right to use a stile into an immature plantation, passing to the left of a pond. Use the rusty hand-gate up some steps and then pass diagonally ahead across the rough drive **E**.

Take the steep path beside the wall on your right, climb a stile and drift gradually right on the obvious path across the moorland. This bends easily left, picking up a line of old wall and fencing on your right. Crest the ridge to find waymarked old stone gateposts on your right. Pass through these and then take the stile on the left, following this walled track (very wet after heavy rain) down to the **Hanging Gate** pub **F**.

Turn right and at the hairpin-left bend, fork right along the 'Quiet Lane', remaining on this to and around a right-hand bend **G** to reach a T-junction. Turn right to return to the car park. ●

Malpas

		GPS waypoints
Start	Malpas	🖈 SJ 487 472
Distance	8½ miles (13.6km)	Ⓐ SJ 484 460
Height gain	395 feet (120m)	Ⓑ SJ 485 443
Approximate time	4 hours	Ⓒ SJ 496 447
Parking	Malpas (free, off High Street)	Ⓓ SJ 510 444
Route terrain	Lanes and field paths, muddy in places. One busy road to cross twice	Ⓔ SJ 522 454
		Ⓕ SJ 526 462
		Ⓖ SJ 517 465
		Ⓗ SJ 505 469
Ordnance Survey maps	Landranger 117 (Chester & Wrexham), Explorer 257 (Crewe & Nantwich)	

This lengthy but undemanding walk explores the countryside of southwest Cheshire to the south and east of Malpas and close to both the Shropshire and Welsh borders. There are fine views looking across to the hills of North Wales.

From its hilltop position Malpas looks across the borderlands to Wales, and the large mound next to the church is the site of a Norman castle that was built to guard the border. The 14th to 15th-century sandstone church, unusually large and imposing for a village church, contains some interesting gargoyles and impressive monuments. Nearby are some black-and-white, half-timbered cottages and houses.

🖈 Start in the village centre at the junction of Church Street and High Street and walk up Church Street to the church. Turn left along a track called Parbutts Lane to a kissing-gate, go through and walk along the left edge of a field. At a crossways by a kissing-gate on the left, turn right, head gently downhill across the field and go through a kissing-gate onto a lane. Keep ahead, follow the lane around a right bend and take the first lane on the left Ⓐ. Follow this winding lane for just over a mile to a T-junction and turn left

Ⓑ along a narrow lane signposted to Lower Wych. Keep ahead through the hamlet, after which the lane ascends and continues to a T-junction.

Turn left; at a public bridleway sign turn right through a gate Ⓒ and bear left across a field. After skirting the left edge of a pond, bear right and make for a gate in the far right corner. Go through, keep ahead across the next field passing to the right of another pond, here veering slightly right to reach and use a flat bridge and bridle-gate in the corner. Walk ahead to pass right of a hollow, then head for the right-hand corner to an open gateway and, beyond, join a hedged old green lane. This can be very muddy in places. Go through a gate, keep ahead and the track bends left to another gate. Go through that one and keep ahead to go through one more onto a road.

Turn left; at a public bridleway sign turn right Ⓓ through a gate and walk along the left edge of a field. Go through another gate, keep along the right edge of the next field and in the corner, go through a gate and cross a bridge over a disused railway. Go through another gate, continue along the right edge of the next three fields, going through two more gates, and in the corner of the last field, go through the bridle-gate and turn left along the field edge. Access the lane near the half-timbered cottage and turn right along it, walking to the nearby **Blue Bell Inn** .

Turn left along the road and walk round a left-hand bend. As this straightens, take the hedged track on the right, walking through to the nearby

very busy A41 road. Cross directly over to join a 'Dead End' tarred lane. Walk to the end of this and use the kissing-gate on the right, heading then along the dirt track across the pasture towards a brick-built church. This is old St Chad's Church, built in 1689 on the site of an earlier timber-framed building. When a new church was built $\frac{1}{2}$ mile away in 1863 to serve the parish of Tushingham, the old church was left standing in the fields on its own.

About 100 yds before reaching the church , turn left and head across the field to a stile. Climb it, keep ahead

Marl hole

across the next field – following Marches Way not Sandstone Trail directions – and in the far corner, go through the right-hand one of two kissing-gates. As you continue across the next field, the Victorian new church of St Chad's is seen over to the left. Climb a stile in the corner, turn left to cross the A41 again, turn right and take the first lane on the left, signposted to Bradley.

At a public footpath sign **G**, at a left-bend after about 400 yds, turn right over a stile and walk the right edge of the field, pass by a field gate and continue alongside the hedge on your right to reach a hand-gate and stile near the field corner. Both these are marked with Marches Way discs, as is most other route furniture for the remainder of this walk. Use either and continue beside a hedge on your right. Take another gate and walk along the field edge just left of Millmoor Farm. Just beyond the buildings, swap sides of the fence via a stile and continue gently downhill keeping the hedge on your left. At a kink in the hedge/fence, swap sides again and look right for a footbridge some 50 yds from the field corner.

Cross the bridge and the nearby stile and walk ahead (not half-right) across the slope to find and use a kissing-gate

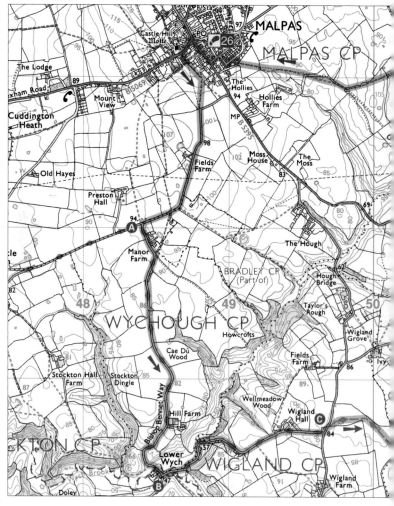

through a hedge. Turn left to a stile, climb this and turn right, dropping to and over a footbridge and stile. Walk to the right, around the snout of a bank to a waymarked stile leading into a grassy path to a lane 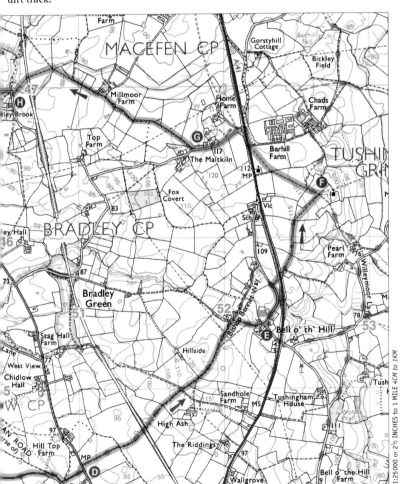.

Turn right down the lane, which bends left and rises up a bank. In about 200 yds, look for a waymarked kissing-gate on the left. Walk diagonally across the field to an offset corner; here bear left to reach to a kissing-gate. Beyond this, crest the rise to reveal a good view of Malpas, then walk ahead down the pasture to use a kissing-gate onto a dirt track.

Turn right, then, as it splays into pasture, turn left alongside a fence. Cross a track, use a kissing-gate and walk ahead to pass a pond on your left before reaching another kissing-gate. From here head half-right towards the church tower. Use a last kissing-gate in the corner, slip between the garages and walk across the parking area and along the tarred access track to a road. Turn left to a T-junction, right to another T-junction and left at this one. At the main road turn right to the town centre.

SCALE 1:25000 or 2½ INCHES to 1 MILE 4CM to 1KM

Tegg's Nose and Macclesfield Forest

		GPS waypoints
Start	Tegg's Nose Country Park, signposted from Macclesfield off Buxton Road	◪ SJ 950 732
		Ⓐ SJ 951 726
Distance	8½ miles (13.7km). Shorter walk 7½ miles (12km)	**Ⓑ** SJ 959 725
		Ⓒ SJ 974 721
Height gain	1,855 feet (565m). Shorter option 1,690 feet (515m)	**Ⓓ** SJ 975 742
		Ⓔ SJ 967 754
Approximate time	4½ hours. Shorter option 4 hours	**Ⓕ** SJ 952 752
		Ⓖ SJ 947 744
Parking	Visitor centre car park (Pay & Display)	
Route terrain	Lanes, rough tracks, field paths. Very hilly with many ups and downs, some steep. Boggy in places in wet weather	
Dog friendly	Obey locally posted signs during the lambing season (on leads Jan–May). There are many stiles on the route	
Ordnance Survey maps	Landranger 118 (Stoke-on-Trent & Macclesfield), Explorer OL24 (The Peak District – White Peak area)	

After an initial descent, rise through Macclesfield Forest to the Forest Chapel. The remainder of the route is undulating and there are likely to be some muddy stretches. The last $1\frac{1}{4}$ miles (2km) is along the Gritstone Trail. The full walk includes a short additional stretch at the end to Tegg's Nose. This is quite a strenuous walk with lots of climbs and descents, sometimes over rough ground, and it is not advisable to attempt it in bad weather, especially in misty conditions, unless experienced in walking in such conditions and able to navigate using a compass.

◪ Start by taking the paved downhill path, signposted Saddlers Way, go through a gate and continue down to a lane. Keep ahead downhill and after going round a sharp left bend in front of the entrance to Clough House **Ⓐ**, the lane becomes first an enclosed track and then an uphill, enclosed path.

The path bends right, heads downhill to ford a stream and continues uphill.

At the top, turn left along another enclosed path and in front of a farm, turn right along a narrow lane. Follow it around a left bend to a metal handgate on the right at a public footpath fingerpost **Ⓑ**.

Enter Macclesfield Forest here, commencing a steady climb through the woods. This part of the forest is a delightful mix of conifers and

Tegg's Nose

broadleaves; most of the rest is conifer plantation, gradually being replanted as broadleaf. The area was a medieval hunting chase; there are still deer here, but they are rarely seen. Keep right at a sign for Forest Chapel to reach a derelict stone barn. Fork half-left to a nearby fingerpost, again for Forest Chapel, indicating a gap stile. The path threads, occasionally steeply up flights of steps, through the woods to reach a handgate into a rough track. Turn right and descend Charity Lane, with marvellous views, right, to Shutlingsloe's sharp summit and ahead across Clough Brook's deep valley to the skyline Cat & Fiddle Inn, second highest in England.

You'll reach Forest Chapel hamlet and the eponymous St Stephen's Chapel. In August each year a rushbearing ceremony is still held here, recalling old times when earthen floors were spread with freshly cut rushes to offer some warmth and fragrancing to the old church. Take a few steps down the rough lane to the right of the chapel and climb the waymarked stone stile **©** on the left. Walk along the enclosed path, climb two stiles in quick succession and walk downhill along the left edge of a field to another stile. Climb that one – a boardwalk enables you to cross a stream and boggy ground – head uphill along the left edge of a field, climb a stile and keep along the left edge of the next field, marked by a low hedgebank. Continue over the brow and descend to a stile.

Climb it, head downhill along the left edge of a field, climb another stile, cross a stream and keep ahead uphill again. Walk past a waymarked post and at the next one, turn left up to another post and bear right towards a farm. Climb a stone stile into the farmyard, turn right by the house and continue along a track to a road. Cross over, climb the stile opposite, walk across a field and go through a gate onto the main Macclesfield-Buxton road.

Cross over, climb a difficult stone stile and then drift slightly right to use another stone stile in the far wall, about 70 yds right of the gateway. Cut across the next field corner, use a ladder stile into a lane and turn left on this. Past Ankers Knowl Farm, the lane bends right and drops steeply **Ⓓ**. Take the rough lane on the left, a waymarked stile leading onto a woodland edge track. Remain on this, keeping outside the woods at a 'Reservoir Circular Walk' fingerpost. Curve left, then sharp right at a boggy bend, continuing via a stile along this old field road beside the woods obscuring Lamaload Reservoir. Leave the stone barn off to your right, steadily climbing the cobbled track past waymarks and posts pointing left to reach a point where the field road bends left.

Leave the field road and walk ahead, climb a stile and keep ahead outside the trees. Use another stile and walk to the left of the knoll with a dead stump on top. A wide grassy path develops, leading directly to the wooded corner ahead. Climb the stile into the trees and walk ahead on the woodland path before dropping down the steepening path by a wood-side wall to reach a hand-gate near the slope foot. Use this and then take the stile on the left, fingerposted for Rainow. Cut up the walled track which curves right to issue onto the reservoir service road **E**.

Turn left, head uphill, follow the track around a left bend and continue along it for a mile as it winds above the Dean valley. Just after passing the fourth house on the left, turn left over a waymarked stone stile **F** just before a cattle-grid and walk uphill across a field. After passing through a wall gap, bear left across the corner of a field, climb a stone stile and head diagonally uphill across the next field. Climb two stiles in quick succession, continue uphill along the right edge of a field and turn right over a ladder stile.

Walk diagonally left to find a high stile near the right-end of the trees. Turn right along the farm lane. Immediately round the next left bend, take the wooden stile on the right beside the Gritstone Trail fingerpost (not the metal stile) and walk beside a wall on your right. Climb a corner stile beneath trees and head half-left to use a kissing-gate. Look slightly right for a distinct gully dropping down to a flat bridge, cross this and keep left to use a stile, then walk to the left of the isolated stone barn to find another stile. Climb this and walk ahead, over the rise to a stile in the top corner **G**.

Turn left alongside the main road. In 50 paces cross carefully to the right to climb narrow steps to a kissing-gate and keep along the right edge of the field.

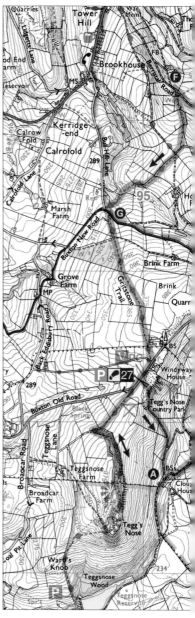

Use another stile and keep ahead, a field path bending very gradually away from new woodland to reach a stile in a cross-wall. From here turn right to use a hand-gate through a wall. Bear half-left to join a well-worn path across pastures and through wall-gaps and over stiles, eventually climbing one to the right of the kennels. Head half-left to use a final

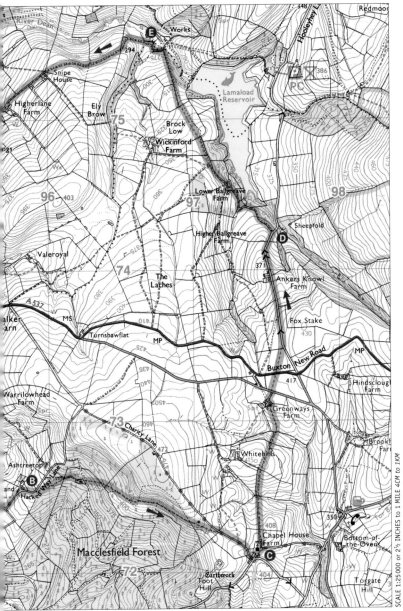

stile in the far corner. Here join the tarred road going downhill to return to the nearby Visitor Centre.

If doing the additional walk to the Tegg's Nose viewpoint – worthwhile not just for the view but also because the area is a maze of old quarry workings – keep ahead past the car park entrance and bear left along a well-surfaced track. Go through a kissing-gate, keep ahead and after going through another gate, the path bends left and heads up, passing by former quarrying equipment, to the viewpoint. From here retrace your steps to the start.

●

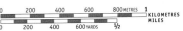

The Etherow and Goyt Valleys

		GPS waypoints
Start	Compstall, Stockport	⬚ SJ 965 908
Distance	10½ miles (16.8km)	**Ⓐ** SJ 979 911
Height gain	1,280 feet (390m)	**Ⓑ** SJ 982 889
Approximate time	5½ hours	**Ⓒ** SJ 992 874
Parking	Etherow Country Park (Pay and Display)	**Ⓓ** SJ 985 863
Route terrain	Lanes, field paths, farm tracks, woodland. Some challenging short ascents, with considerable ups and downs along the way	**Ⓔ** SJ 966 873
Ordnance Survey maps	Landranger 109 (Manchester), Explorer OL1 (The Peak District – Dark Peak area)	

The rivers Etherow and Goyt are headwaters of the River Mersey. They drain the high moorlands of the Dark Peak through magnificent wooded gorges that curl below gritstone edges and sinuous ridges marking the edge of the Peak District. This walk explores these attributes, revealing magnificent views across Cheshire's hilly eastern fringe.

Compstall stands beside lodges created to supply mills built by the industrialist George Andrew in the 1820s. Parts of the mills survive beside the Etherow; the rest of his private estate here forms the heart of one of Britain's first Country Parks, established in 1968.

🖉 Face the Visitor Centre and turn right along the path for Ernocroft Wood, passing terraces before becoming a quiet tarred lane. The channel on your right was a tub-boat canal, used to move coal from adit mines in the woods to the mill complex.

At the spectacular weir, cross the bridge and fork right 50 yds beyond it into the nature reserve. At the fork keep left for 'Picnic Site', starting a long, steady climb through Ernocroft Wood, renowned for its wide range of wildflowers and birds. At the junction beyond a cross-path, turn left for 'Glossop Road'; the path rises to a gateway onto the A626 **Ⓐ**.

Turn right to a bus stop in 200 yds. Look left for the gate-side stile into an old sunken track; this bends left and rises through a fold of cottages at Ernocroft. Turn right up the lane and remain with this for ½ mile, drinking in the great views across Manchester and Cheshire. At the T-junction, cross into the rough track opposite, descending into a deep little valley and the hamlet of Hollywood End.

Turn left, cross the brook and take the path, right, for Marple. This shortly winds across a field; at the far side turn left alongside the broken wall to a stile into a sleeve of trees. Keep ahead from the far end to a straggly old hedge; turn right beyond this up a field track, use the stile and bear right towards the distant white-painted house. Turn left up the green track, jig through the pen at the top and keep left to the isolated church above Mellor **B**.

An information board reveals some of the remarkable finds made on a long-term archaeological dig of this hill-fort and Bronze Age site. Walk down the lane; where it bends right, fork left through the green gate (not the ornate gates), slipping by the farmhouse and into a field-foot path. Persevere beyond a step-stile to find a handgate on your right; from here trace the well-worn path through to Moorend, emerging on a lane beyond the **Oddfellows** pub. The way is straight over and along the narrow walled pathway. Enter the steep field at the end (not the garden) and climb the well-defined path ahead over a stile, curving left with the wall to the farm on the skyline. Pass between the

houses; at the far side of the cobbled yard turn right up an enclosed path to a concreted track and turn left to the cross-lane.

Go straight over, joining the rough Primrose Lane. In about 600 yds, just before trees, turn right **C** along another old moorland road, Black Lane. Magnificent views stretch across this corrugated countryside to Kinder's great plateau. At the junction turn left and pass by 'Three Chimneys' into a rough lane. In 150 yds, go right at the faded footpath sign down a walled track. Turn left along the lane near the house; as it bends right go ahead over stiles beside two successive field gates to reach an isolated footpath fingerpost. Keep left, following the path around the rough snout of the hill. At the gate beyond the broiler house turn right to a lane. Turn left to reach pretty, secluded Brook Bottom **D**.

The Goyt Way eases down the rough track just past the **Fox Inn**, charting a way within the trees at the lip of a precipitous clough sliced into the ridge.

The old bridge in Brabyns Park

Pass beneath the railway and continue until the cobbles become tarmac. Turn right along the lane (Goyt Way), crossing the railway to reach Greenclough Farm. Cross the stone bridge and turn left; in 100 yds take the higher path, soon leaving the woods to parallel the railway embankment. At the fork keep left, presently walking in front of Richmond (or Windybottom) Farm, then through a tunnel beneath the railway. Stick with this old lane beside the Goyt to reach a footpath, left, for Strines, immediately crossing the graceful Roman Bridge packhorse bridge **E**.

Curl left off it; just after the stone mounting block, take the stepped path on the right, climbing steeply through the woods to a gap-stile into a road. Turn right and in 300 yds take the fingerposted path left [just past No.94], rising to the Peak Forest Canal. Turn right along this wildflower-rich towpath. At the next roving bridge swap sides, remaining on the towpath to reach the junction with the Macclesfield Canal. Our way is to the right, so cross the bridge and drop beside the top flight of Marple Locks.

Stay with the towpath across two main roads, all the way to lock 2, where a gap-stile on the right beckons. Drop down wooden steps and turn left, falling on a ledged path through the woods to gain the edge of meadows. Turn left along the Goyt Way; at the riverbank, turn right and walk upstream to reach a surfaced track. Turn left across the nearby bridge over the Goyt, a notable cast-iron structure dated 1813. Remain with the track to the main road at the **George Inn**. Turn left, cross the bridge over the Etherow and walk past the mill to find the car park on your right.   ●

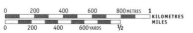

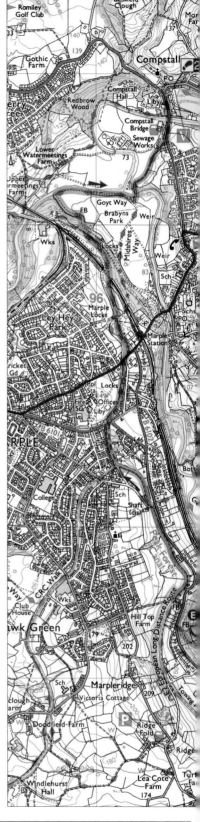

Further Information

Walking Safety

Although the reasonably gentle countryside that is the subject of this book offers no real dangers to walkers at any time of the year, it is still advisable to take sensible precautions and follow certain well-tried guidelines.

Always take with you both warm and waterproof clothing and sufficient food and drink. Wear suitable footwear, such as strong walking boots or shoes that give a good grip over stony ground, on slippery slopes and in muddy conditions. Try to obtain a local weather forecast and bear it in mind before you start. Do not be afraid to abandon your proposed route and return to your starting point in the event of a sudden and unexpected deterioration in the weather.

All the walks described in this book will be safe to do, given due care and respect, even during the winter. Indeed, a crisp, fine winter day often provides perfect walking conditions, with firm ground underfoot and a clarity unique to this time of the year. The most difficult hazard likely to be encountered is mud, especially when walking along woodland and field paths, farm tracks and bridleways – the latter in particular can often get churned up by cyclists and horses. In summer, an additional difficulty may be narrow and overgrown paths, particularly along the edges of cultivated fields. Neither should constitute a major problem provided that the appropriate footwear is worn.

The Ramblers

No organisation works more actively to protect and extend the rights and interests of walkers in the countryside than the Ramblers. Its aims are clear: to foster a greater knowledge, love and care of the countryside; to assist in the protection and enhancement of public rights of way and areas of natural beauty; to work for greater public access to the countryside; and to encourage more people to take up rambling as a healthy, recreational leisure activity.

It was founded in 1935 as the Ramblers' Association and has played a key role in preserving and developing the national footpath network, supporting the creation of national parks and encouraging the designation and waymarking of long-distance routes.

Our freedom of access to the countryside, now enshrined in legislation, is still in its early years and requires constant vigilance. But over and above this there will always be the problem of footpaths being illegally obstructed, disappearing through lack of use, or being extinguished by housing or road construction.

It is to meet such problems and dangers that the Ramblers exists and represents the interests of all walkers. The address to write to for information on the Ramblers and how to become a member is given on page 95.

Walkers and the Law

The Countryside and Rights of Way Act (CRoW Act 2000) extends the rights of access previously enjoyed by walkers in England and Wales. Implementation of these rights began on 19 September 2004. The Act amends existing legislation and for the first time provides access on foot to certain types of land – defined as mountain, moor, heath, down and registered common land.

Where You Can Go
Rights of Way

Prior to the introduction of the CRoW Act, walkers could only legally access the countryside along public rights of way. These are either 'footpaths' (for walkers only) or 'bridleways' (for walkers, riders on horseback and pedal cyclists). A third category called 'Byways open to all traffic' (BOATs), is used by motorised vehicles as

Countryside Access Charter

Your rights of way are:

- public footpaths – on foot only. Sometimes waymarked in yellow
- bridle-ways – on foot, horseback and pedal cycle. Sometimes waymarked in blue
- byways (usually old roads), most 'roads used as public paths' and, of course, public roads – all traffic has the right of way

Use maps, signs and waymarks to check rights of way. Ordnance Survey Explorer and Landranger maps show most public rights of way

On rights of way you can:

- take a pram, pushchair or wheelchair if practicable
- take a dog (on a lead or under close control)
- take a short route round an illegal obstruction or remove it sufficiently to get past

You have a right to go for recreation to:

- public parks and open spaces – on foot
- most commons near older towns and cities – on foot and sometimes on horseback
- private land where the owner has a formal agreement with the local authority

In addition you can use the following by local or established custom or consent, but ask for advice if you are unsure:

- many areas of open country, such as moorland, fell and coastal areas, especially those in the care of the National Trust, and some commons
- some woods and forests, especially those owned by the Forestry Commission
- country parks and picnic sites
- most beaches
- canal towpaths
- some private paths and tracks Consent sometimes extends to horse-riding and cycling

For your information:

- county councils and London boroughs maintain and record rights of way, and register commons
- obstructions, dangerous animals, harassment and misleading signs on rights of way are illegal and you should report them to the county council
- paths across fields can be ploughed, but must normally be reinstated within two weeks
- landowners can require you to leave land to which you have no right of access
- motor vehicles are normally permitted only on roads, byways and some 'roads used as public paths'

well as those using non-mechanised transport. Mainly they are green lanes, farm and estate roads, although occasionally they will be found crossing mountainous area.

Rights of way are marked on Ordnance Survey maps. Look for the green broken lines on the Explorer maps, or the red dashed lines on Landranger maps.

The term 'right of way' means exactly what it says. It gives a right of passage over what, for the most part, is private land. Under pre-CRoW legislation walkers were required to keep to the line of the right of way and not stray onto land on either side. If you did inadvertently wander off the right of way, either because of faulty map reading or because the route was not clearly indicated on the ground, you were

technically trespassing.

Local authorities have a legal obligation to ensure that rights of way are kept clear and free of obstruction, and are signposted where they leave metalled roads. The duty of local authorities to install signposts extends to the placing of signs along a path or way, but only where the authority considers it necessary to have a signpost or waymark to assist persons unfamiliar with the locality.

The New Access Rights
Access Land
As well as being able to walk on existing rights of way, under the new legislation you now have access to large areas of open land. You can of course continue to use

rights of way footpaths to cross this land, but the main difference is that you can now lawfully leave the path and wander at will, but only in areas designated as access land.

Where to Walk

Areas now covered by the new access rights – Access Land – are shown on Ordnance Survey Explorer maps bearing the access land symbol on the front cover.

'Access Land' is shown on Ordnance Survey maps by a light yellow tint surrounded by a pale orange border. New orange coloured 'i' symbols on the maps will show the location of permanent access information boards installed by the access authorities.

Restrictions

The right to walk on access land may lawfully be restricted by landowners. Landowners can, for any reason, restrict access for up to 28 days in any year. They cannot however close the land:

- on bank holidays;
- for more than four Saturdays and Sundays in a year;
- on any Saturday from 1 June to 11 August; or
- on any Sunday from 1 June to the end of September.

They have to provide local authorities with five working days' notice before the date of closure unless the land involved is an area of less than five hectares or the closure is for less than four hours. In these cases landowners only need to provide two hours' notice.

Whatever restrictions are put into place on access land they have no effect on existing rights of way, and you can continue to walk on them.

Dogs

Dogs can be taken on access land, but must be kept on leads of two metres or less between 1 March and 31 July, and at all times where they are near livestock. In addition landowners may impose a ban on all dogs from fields where lambing takes place for up to six weeks in any year. Dogs may be banned from moorland used for grouse shooting and breeding for up to five years.

In the main, walkers following the routes in this book will continue to follow existing rights of way, but a knowledge and understanding of the law as it affects walkers, plus the ability to distinguish access land marked on the maps, will enable anyone who wishes to depart from paths that cross access land either to take a shortcut, to enjoy a view or to explore.

General Obstructions

Obstructions can sometimes cause a problem on a walk and the most common of these is where the path across a field has been ploughed over. It is legal for a farmer to plough up a path provided that it is restored within two weeks. This does not always happen and you are faced with the dilemma of following the line of the path, even if this means treading on crops, or walking round the edge of the field. Although the latter course of action seems the most sensible, it does mean that you would be trespassing.

Other obstructions can vary from overhanging vegetation to wire fences across the path, locked gates or even a cattle feeder on the path.

Use common sense. If you can get round the obstruction without causing damage, do so. Otherwise only remove as much of the obstruction as is necessary to secure passage.

If the right of way is blocked and cannot be followed, there is a long-standing view that in such circumstances there is a right to deviate, but this cannot wholly be relied on. Although it is accepted in law that highways (and that includes rights of way) are for the public service, and if the usual track is impassable, it is for the general good that people should be entitled to pass into another line. However, this should not be taken as indicating a right to deviate whenever a way becomes impassable. If in doubt, retreat.

Report obstructions to the local authority and/or the Ramblers.

Useful Organisations

Campaign to Protect Rural England
128 Southwark Street, London SE1 0SW
Tel. 020 7981 2800
www.cpre.org.uk

Cheshire East Council
PROW Section, Phoenix House, Clough
Road, Winsford, Cheshire CW7 4BD
Tel. 01606 271 830
www.cheshireeast.gov.uk

Cheshire West & Chester
PROW Section (Highways),
Nicholas Street, Chester CH1 2NP
Tel. 01244 973 237
www.cheshirewestandchester.gov.uk

English Heritage
Customer Services Department,
PO Box 569, Swindon SN2 2YP
Tel. 0870 333 1181
www.english-heritage.org.uk

Forestry Commission England
Great Eastern House, Tenison Road,
Cambridge CB1 2DU
Tel. 01223 314546
www.forestry.gov.uk

Long Distance Walkers' Association
www.ldwa.org.uk

National Trust
PO Box 39, Warrington ,WA5 7WD
Tel. 0870 458 4000
www.nationaltrust.org.uk

Natural England
1 East Parade, Sheffield S1 2ET
Tel. 0114 241 8920
www.naturalengland.org.uk

North West Tourist Board
www.visitnorthwest.com

Ordnance Survey
Customer Service Centre,
Romsey Road,
Maybush, Southampton
SO16 4GU
Tel. 08456 05 05 05 (Helpline)
www.ordnancesurvey.co.uk

the Ramblers
2nd Floor, Camelford House, 87-90 Albert
Embankment, London SE1 7TW
Tel. 020 7339 8500
www.ramblers.org.uk

Tourist Information Centres
Tourist Information Centres are usually
open daily between 10.00 and 17.30.
Chester: 01244 402111
Congleton: 01260 271095
Ellesmere Port & Neston: 0151 356 5562
Macclesfield: 01625 504114
Nantwich: 01270 537359
Northwich: 01606 353534
Runcorn: 0151 907 8303
Warrington: 01925 428585

 Ordnance Survey maps of Cheshire

The area of Cheshire is covered by
Ordnance survey 1:50 000 scale (1¼
inches to 1 mile or 2cm to 1km) scale
Landranger map sheets 108, 109, 117,118.

To examine Cheshire in more detail and
especially if you are planning walks,
Explorer maps at 1:25 000 (2½ inches to
1 mile or 4cm to 1km) scale are ideal:

OL1 (The Peak District – Dark Peak area)
OL24 (The Peak District – White Peak area)
257 (Crewe & Nantwich)
266 (Wirral & Chester)
267 (Northwich & Delamere Forest)
268 (Wilmslow, Macclesfield & Congleton)
275 (Liverpool)
276 (Bolton, Wigan & Warrington)

To get to Cheshire, use Ordnance Survey
OS Travel Map – Route Great Britain at
1:625 000 scale (4cm to 25km or 1 inch to
10 miles) or OS Travel Map – Road No. 4
(Northern England) at 1:250 000 scale
(1cm to 2.5km or 1 inch to 4 miles).

Ordance Survey maps and guides are
available from most booksellers, stationers
and newsagents.

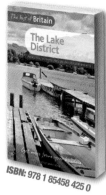